Cutright, Melitta J., 1944-
The National PTA talks to parents

The National PTA Talks to Parents

The National PTA Talks to Parents

How to Get the Best Education for Your Child

Melitta J. Cutright, Ph.D.

DOUBLEDAY

NEW YORK LONDON TORONTO
SYDNEY AUCKLAND

To Elisabeth
and
the 40 million other students in our nation's public schools

Published by Doubleday, a division of
Bantam Doubleday Dell Publishing Group, Inc.
666 Fifth Avenue, New York, New York 10103

Doubleday and the portrayal of an anchor
with a dolphin are trademarks of Doubleday,
a division of Bantam Doubleday Dell
Publishing Group, Inc.

PTA®, Parent-Teacher Association® and the PTA oak tree logo are registered service marks of the National PTA.

Library of Congress Cataloging-in-Publication Data

Cutright, Melitta J., 1944–
The National PTA talks to parents : how to get the best education for your child / by Melitta J. Cutright. — 1st ed.
p. cm.
Bibliography: p.
Includes index.
ISBN 0-385-24702-8 — ISBN 0-385-24703-6 (pbk.)
1. Home and school—United States. 2. Education—United States—Parent participation. I. Title.
LC225.3.C88 1989 89-31156
370.19'31—dc19 CIP

Book Design by Robert Bull Design

Printed in the United States of America
September 1989
First Edition

FG

CONTENTS

PREFACE

FOR MORE THAN ninety years the National PTA (National Congress of Parents and Teachers) has helped parents gain the best possible education for their children. We have encouraged individual parents to take an active part in their child's education and to work with others in their community to strengthen their local schools. In order to provide all youngsters with a high-quality education, we have sought improvements in our schools, spoken out for adequate funding for public education and worked to assure that public funds are used only for public schools.

In addition, the National PTA has played an important part in teaching generations of Americans to be better parents; in establishing child labor laws and the juvenile justice system; in creating a national public health service; and in developing school hot lunch programs, drug and alcohol abuse prevention programs, the field tests of the Salk polio vaccine, AIDS education projects for home and school and other programs. The PTA is the oldest and largest organization working solely on behalf of children and youth.

Parents have come to look to their PTA for advice on

how to get the best education for their child, on how to be better parents and on how to protect the health, safety and welfare of their child. In order to reach more parents and improve education for all children, the PTA decided to write a book suggesting practical ways of working with your child, with school staff and with other parents. Information in this book is based on educational research and the experience of generations of PTA members and leaders.

This guide will help you get the best education for your child, whether or not your school has a PTA. If you do belong to a PTA (parent-teacher association) or PTSA (parent-teacher-student association), you will learn that you are part of a nationwide network of parents, teachers, grandparents, school staff members and other concerned people, all working together to improve education. If your school does not have a PTA, why not consider starting one, or converting the parent organization in your school into a PTA? For information about how to organize a PTA, contact your state PTA or the National PTA. Its address is 700 North Rush Street, Chicago, IL 60611-2571.

I would like to thank many people for their help in preparing this book. Among them are PTA leaders, including Manya Ungar, Jean Dye, Ann Lynch, Anne Campbell, Millie Waterman and Grace Foster. A special thanks goes to the staff of the National PTA. Among the current and former staff members who worked on this project or who prepared material used in this book are Robert Woerner, Denise Carter, Victoria Andrews, Gloria Ryan, Laura Abraham, Jeanne Koepsell, Mary Munday, Osa Theus and Monica Culpepper. Thanks should also be given to my mother, Madeleine, who read draft after draft; to my husband, Jim; and to my editor, Alison Brown Cerier.

A final thank you goes to the more than 6.6 million PTA members today and to the millions of past members who have worked long and hard to improve the lives of children and youth in America.

AUTHOR'S NOTE:

Although most of the information in this book applies equally to boys and girls, "she" is used in odd-numbered chapters and "he" in even-numbered ones.

CHAPTER

1

You Can Make a Difference

"THE DIFFERENCE BETWEEN a good school and a great school is the parents," says Bessie McLemore, principal of Fulton High School in Atlanta, Georgia. It sounds simple, but it's true—you can improve your child's ability to learn and to achieve success in school by helping her at home and keeping a close watch on her schooling, both of which show that you value education. And you can improve her school just by playing an active role there.

Whether you are a middle-class suburbanite, a parent living in the slums of a major city or a resident of a rural area, whether you are a doctor or a dishwasher, your involvement will mean that your child will learn more and do better in school. In fact, children whose parents are actively involved in their education often score higher on achievement tests than do others who have more ability or greater social and cultural advantages, but whose parents are not involved. A report issued in 1986 by the Department of Education confirmed that "what parents do to help their children learn is more important to academic success than how well-off the family is."

More than fifty major research studies of the role of parents in education, summarized by Anne Henderson in *The Evidence Continues to Grow*, have shown that:

- Parents' involvement increases their children's achievement.
- Parents' involvement continues to be important even when students are in high school.
- It isn't enough for parents just to be active in their children's education at home—they must participate at all levels in the schools if the schools are to be of high quality.
- Parents don't have to be well educated to help their children improve academically.
- Minority and low-income children gain most from having their parents take an active part in their schooling.

You don't have to invest a great deal of time. Half an hour a day reading and talking to your child will make a difference. A few minutes each evening skimming and discussing her homework and the exams and other work she brings home will make a difference. A brief conversation now and then showing your child that her education is important to you will make a difference. An hour or two a year talking to your child's teacher will make a difference. A couple of hours a week or even once a month volunteering in your child's school will make a difference, and so will attending PTA meetings and supporting PTA efforts to improve the schools. In fact, one study found that simply having an active PTA in your school will increase student achievement.

Maybe you are already trying to help your child at home but aren't sure if you are giving her the best assistance. Maybe you want to get more involved in her school but don't know how. In this book you will find practical suggestions for helping your child learn at home and for getting more involved in your school. You'll get help in finding your way around your local school and in assessing how well your child is doing in school. You'll learn how to recognize a good teacher and an effective school. You'll find out how to get assistance for a special child, and how to work with the school to keep your child healthy. You'll learn about the current "educational excellence," or reform movement, and how to make your voice heard so that you can get what you want for your child.

You'll discover why you need to raise your sights—why worrying about only your own child and her school isn't enough—and why you need to work to assure that *all* children receive the education they need. You'll read about programs and projects of PTAs across the nation that your PTA can duplicate. Finally, you'll be encouraged to draw up an action plan for taking charge of your child's education.

Before you begin, though, take a close look at how involved you already are in your child's education by filling out a "Report Card for Parents." As you study the results, think about how you can take a more active part in your child's education.

Will Your School Welcome Your Involvement?

A survey by the National Education Association (NEA) found that over 90 percent of teachers want more parent involvement. In fact, parent indifference often rates above low teacher salaries as a cause of dissatisfaction for our nation's teachers. If you ask principals or superintendents whether they invite parents to be actively involved in their schools, most likely they will say yes. If you ask parents if they'd like to be more actively involved, once again the answer will be overwhelmingly yes. So if parents, teachers and school administrators want parents to be more actively involved in their children's schooling, why aren't they?

The answer is complicated. Many parents don't know how to be involved or don't think that they have the time. Others feel that they don't have enough education or so-

A REPORT CARD FOR PARENTS

Grade yourself with an A, B, C, D or F on how well you help your child learn. An A means that you are very actively involved in your child's education. An F means that you have a lot of work to do.

Do I:

____ Maintain a good working relationship with my child's teacher?

____ Show my child that I value education in general and her education in particular by talking about the importance of education in her life and mine?

____ Attend all parent-teacher conferences, PTA meetings and school events, such as open houses, plays and band concerts?

____ Read to my child every day if she is too young to read on her own?

____ Encourage my child to read on her own, or read jointly with her and take her to the library?

____ Provide a quiet time and place for my child to study and read?

____ Insist that my child do all assigned homework?

____ Make sure that my child attends school every day, if possible?

____ Expect my child to do her best in all subjects, including math, science, art, music and physical education?

____ Take an interest in what interests my child?

____ Show pleasure and pride in my child's accomplishments?

____ Encourage my child to do her best without putting undue pressure on her to succeed in scholastic, athletic or extracurricular pursuits?

____ Understand school rules, policies and budget, and make my views known about important educational issues?

____ Secure special assistance if my child needs it?

____ Limit television watching and plan other individual and family activities?

____ See that my child gets lots of exercise, nutritious food and plenty of rest?

____ Make sure that my child has free time to play and enjoy herself, and insist that she not fill all her out-of-school hours with activities?

____ Respect my child and her feelings as I do those of my friends and other family members?

phistication to understand school problems and are afraid that educators will find them stupid. Many parents feel intimidated or unwelcome in schools.

In the past, many educators tried to shut parents out of the schools. "Leave education to the professionals—the teachers and principals and other school staff," they seemed to be saying. Many school administrators felt that they didn't need parents' support and tried to convince parents not to "interfere." Over the last decade, though, most educators have begun to recognize the importance of parent involvement. They now realize that children won't learn as well and schools won't function as well unless parents and schools work together. The tightening of school funds and criticism of public schools have shown administrators and teachers that without parent assistance, school budgets will not pass and other support will not be forthcoming. And educators have come to learn that parents are less likely to be active supporters if they have no role in the schools.

Thus, in the past few years, the welcome mat has gone out for parents in most of our nation's public schools. However, many parents are so busy that they aren't responding. Also, some parents who do enter the schools are finding that a subtle resistance still exists and that only certain types of parent involvement are welcomed.

Parents who work actively with their children at home and also with teachers are usually greeted with open arms by the school. Parents who support the school by attending school performances and volunteering to tutor students, grade papers or chaperon class trips, as well as those who organize with other parents to pass tax increases for the schools, are certainly appreciated. But parents who seek to participate in policy formulation may raise the hackles of school administrators and teachers. Parents can assume a decision-making role in textbook selection committees, in teams that help set goals for the school or in a school committee that, under a currently popular educational reform called "school-based" or "school-site management," helps make major decisions about the operation of the school.

Some teachers and principals fear that if parents are allowed to help make decisions, they will try to run the school. In particular, many educators are afraid that the only parents who will attempt to influence school decisions will be those with an ax to grind. For this reason, some educators react negatively to any hint of parental criticism or to the suggestion that parents play an active decision-making role in the school. Such defensiveness has discouraged many parents from becoming active in their schools. If you are greeted with distrust when you try to get more involved in your school, don't be discouraged. If you are patient, persistent and diplomatic, you will probably find that in time your school staff will become more open to your participation.

PTAs in Action

Most state and many council and local PTAs have parent involvement projects. For example:

- The Northeast Area PTA Council in Greenville, South Carolina, developed a project called "Parents as Partners in Education." Speakers suggested concrete ways parents could become more involved in their children's education at home and at school. The PTA helped teachers with classroom needs, for example, by lining up parent helpers for special science projects. The PTA also educated parents about the opportunities for vocational education offered by the school's career center.
- The School Six PTA in Linden, New Jersey, helped working parents become active by asking them to pay a visit to their school during their lunch hour. Through the "Take a Parent to Lunch" program, parents of two classes were in-

vited to eat with their children and classmates. The principal and teachers moved about the lunchroom getting to know parents and discussing school and class projects.

• The Ben Franklin Elementary PTA in Sioux Falls, South Dakota, sponsors two events that never fail to get a great turnout: "Donuts with Dads" and "Mums for Moms." School and PTA leaders talk informally with the parents about the school and about getting more involved in their children's education.

• When a new superintendent of schools was hired, the Winston Churchill PTA in Palatine, Illinois, invited parents and community members to meet him and to participate in a question-and-answer session.

• Like thousands of other PTAs, the Shawnee Mission East PTA in Kansas sponsors an annual Back-to-School Night, but what makes this event different is that as many as two thousand people attend. The PTA also sponsors a picnic for incoming students and their parents, and frequent coffees with the principal, to which all parents are invited.

• The Woodland Forrest Elementary PTA in Tuscaloosa, Alabama, welcomes new parents by pairing them with a family that is actively involved with the school.

• The Monticello Middle School PTA in Cleveland Heights, Ohio, held a Back-to-School Day. They invited parents and others from the community to visit classes, tour the school and meet with school counselors and other staff to discuss the school and how to increase the parent and community role in education. To make visitors feel like students again, the staff gave a homework assignment, which most participants filled out and returned.

• The Crabapple Middle School PTA in Roswell, Georgia, created the "Community Partnership Program" to involve parents, businesses, fraternal organizations and community members more closely with the school. A hundred or so people were assigned homerooms and asked to visit often to share their interests and expertise with students and school staff.

• The Forest North Elementary PTA in Austin, Texas, encouraged senior citizens to become active in its school. Through its "Partners in Education" program, the school was "adopted" by a nearby retirement home. The seniors volunteered in the school and got to know the students, while the students provided their adopted grandparents with lots of love.

CHAPTER 2

Getting Ready for School

YOU ARE YOUR child's first and best teacher. In the four or five years before children begin their formal education, they learn an incredible amount—physical skills like crawling and walking, language skills including talking and understanding thousands of words, problem-solving skills, information about themselves and the world.

A great deal of what they learn comes from watching their parents, siblings, friends, baby-sitters or child-care providers. Yet, according to a 1986 U.S. Department of Education report entitled *What Works,* the average American mother spends less than half an hour a day talking or reading with her children, and fathers spend less than fifteen minutes.

Most children learn even when their parents don't consciously realize that they are teaching, but if you actively stimulate your child and provide opportunities for a wide variety of activities, he will learn faster. He will also be better prepared to start school and more likely to do well once he gets there.

Off to a Good Start

"Talking to your children is probably the most important thing that you can do to give them a good start toward lifelong learning," says former National PTA president Manya Ungar. From the time children are born, both mothers and fathers should talk to them, listen to them, sing to them, play with them, laugh with them, tell them stories and show them that they are loved and respected. "Take time, make time for your children. The hours you spend with them when they are young will pay off when they are in school and when they are grown," Ungar advises.

From his birth on, you should also begin reading to your child. You will soon find that even a baby responds to your voice and enjoys rhythms and rhymes. And once you begin reading to your child each day for fifteen minutes or more, reading will become a special time for you both to enjoy.

Probably long before your child is a year old, he will become interested in looking at picture books and in touching the pages, especially if the books are the "touch and feel" kind, with different textures and objects to scratch and smell or move around. Talk with him about the story and the characters, trying to link the stories to things he already knows, to his everyday life. For example, when you read to your toddler about Jack and Jill, you might ask him if he remembers some of *his* recent falls. As your child gets older, ask him questions about what you are reading, especially questions that require some thought. For example, ask him to imagine what is going to happen in a story, why characters acted as they did or what he would have done in the same situation.

Although children love to hear their favorite stories read over and over, be sure to have a variety of reading materials. Buy your child books of his own and set up a special shelf or bookcase for them. Take him to the library. Teach him to love, value and take care of books. Most of all, read, read, read to him as much as you can.

Also, give your young child crayons and encourage him to draw or scribble. Studies of even very young children show that their scribbling has meaning for them. Such pretend writing sets the stage for later language skills, which is particularly important, since writing, speaking and reading are the foundation for what children learn in school or out.

In addition to speaking with and reading to your child, you should also help him with his physical development. Encourage him to crawl and walk, to stretch and roll around. Within limits of safety, let him move about and explore, touching and playing with toys and household objects like pots, pans and wooden spoons. The more your child moves about and explores, the more curiosity he will have, and curiosity is the best motivator for learning. Work with him on puzzles, games and blocks, all of which develop the small-motor coordination needed for holding a pencil and other school skills.

Take your child with you to such "adult" places as the post office, bank and cleaners. Talk to him about where and why you are going, and what the people in these places are doing. Help him count everyday things: the number of trees on your street, the blue cars in the parking lot, the aisles in the grocery store. Take him on walks, and to such "kid" places as the zoo, the playground or the swimming pool. Call attention to sounds, such as a cash register ringing, birds chirping, workers tearing up a street or the girl next door practicing her violin. Help him identify and mimic sounds. All these experiences will stimulate your child's imagination as well as show him what other people are like.

Take your child for regular medical checkups. Pay special attention to his hearing and vision, because you are more likely to notice any problems than is the doctor. Does your child respond from a very early age to sounds? Does he hear out of both ears or does he always turn one way toward a sound? Does he have frequent ear infections? Do his eyes "track" correctly, i.e., do they move the same way when focusing on an object? Does he squint or turn his head to use one eye more than the other? If you suspect any problems, tell your doctor immediately. Hearing and vision problems can greatly limit how well a child learns, and many of these problems are best treated when the child is young. Some problems like amblyopia, a muscle weakness known as "lazy eye," can lead to loss of sight in the affected eye if not treated when the child is young.

Positive Discipline

Teachers report that many children are starting school with little self-discipline. Not only does self-discipline influence children's classroom behavior, but it is also one of the basic requirements for achievement. These teachers believe that school discipline will never improve unless discipline at home improves first. How you discipline and treat your child at home will, in large measure, determine whether he develops self-discipline.

Discipline is one of the most difficult problems parents face. To many people, discipline means verbal or physical punishment, shouting or scolding children for misbehaving. Actually, discipline should be a positive way to help children achieve self-control, to guide them toward acceptable behavior and to teach them to make wise decisions when dealing with life's problems.

Rather than looking for misbehavior to punish, you need to teach your child which behavior is allowed and not allowed, and why. For example, calmly ask your child, "Please pick up your clothes from the floor so I can vacuum in here" instead of screaming, "I'm sick and tired of you always throwing your clothes on the floor! Don't ever let me catch you doing it again!" You will find that discipline works best if you stress "do's" rather than "don'ts." Regularly praise your child for good behavior; catch him being good instead of just reprimanding him when he does something bad.

TEN ACTIVITIES FOR PRESCHOOLERS

1. Help your child make a folder for his "best" artwork. Let him select what to include and encourage him to show his work to family and friends.
2. Cook together. Cooking teaches about measuring, fractions, coordination and time. Let even a young child help mix, break eggs and spread peanut butter or icing.
3. Give your child a pen and ask him to circle all the *p*'s on a page of the newspaper. Or cut up comic strips and encourage him to arrange the frames to make a story.
4. Play card and board games.
5. Help your child write a book. Take down a story as he tells it, spreading the narration out over several sheets of paper. Then have him draw pictures to decorate his work. Staple the sheets into a book and display it for all to see. Or help your youngster tape-record his story.
6. Give your child jumbo chalk and have him draw pictures and write letters or words on the sidewalk. He will particularly enjoy drawing or writing greetings before guests arrive.
7. Play "rhyme off." Say a simple word like "cat" and ask your child to say a rhyming word. Then take turns with new words.
8. Assemble a dress-up box with hats, fake fur capes and other items of clothing. Tell or read a story about fire fighters, doctors or superheroes, and then see what your child can put on to mimic those characters.
9. Ask your child to help empty the dishwasher or dish drainer. Have him sort the silverware or count the cups.
10. Turn a walk into an exploration. Look for objects that start with various letters or for leaves, bark and rocks to collect and study. Listen for sounds. Count the light poles and station wagons, or try to guess where all the motorists are going.

Studies have shown that physical punishment such as spanking and slapping, or verbal abuse like shouting and belittling are ineffective methods of discipline. They may seem to get results for the moment, but in the long run they are more harmful than helpful. Physical punishment demoralizes and humiliates children, causing them to develop low self-esteem. And it doesn't help them develop the self-discipline they will need as they grow up.

Taming the TV Monster

Another tough problem for most parents is what to do about television. Television has a marvelous ability to entertain and to educate, and more than one generation of American children have been delighted, stimulated and intrigued by shows like "Sesame Street," "Mister Rogers' Neighborhood" and "Captain Kangaroo." But how much television is too much? And what effects will all the commercials and violence have on the many children who watch each day?

Though experts advise parents never to prop young children in front of the TV while fixing dinner, sitting down with the paper or talking on the phone, the reality is that all parents do this from time to time. Still, try not to make a habit of using even good TV shows as a baby-sitter. Television is most useful and least harmful to children in small doses—not more than an hour a day for preschoolers—and when it is shared and discussed with parents. Watching television with your young child will give you a lot to talk about together, since even very young children delight in explaining to confused parents or grandparents that the tall, yellow one is Bert, and the short, orange one is Ernie.

Most parents are aware of the potential dangers of letting young children watch violent TV shows, but many don't realize that violence isn't the only problem. By its very nature, television watching is passive. Too often both children and adults turn off their brains when they turn on the set. Some people have called television the "plug-in drug." Young children have special problems because they can't figure out what on TV is real and what isn't. They also can't understand the purpose of commercials.

Some of the passivity and the question of what is real

NATIONAL PTA'S DISCIPLINE TIPS

- Set a good example. Children learn more from how parents act than from what they say.
- Set limits on behavior, but be careful not to make too many rules. Generally, young children need more rules than older ones do.
- Avoid constant criticism and nagging. Try to ignore unwanted behavior unless it is destructive or dangerous. Instead, offer praise and positive suggestions, which foster self-esteem.
- Take time to listen to your child, especially if there is a problem or a rule he wants to discuss.
- Encourage your child's independence. For example, let him select his own clothes and dress himself. Help him realize that he can cope without you.
- Let your child help make family rules and decisions since he will be less likely to break rules he has helped to make.
- Be consistent. A few rules that are always enforced are more effective than many rules that are enforced only sporadically.
- Act quickly when your child misbehaves. Don't let a problem fester.
- Be flexible. Some rules need to be changed. Be especially careful to eliminate rules that are no longer necessary as your child grows older. This will encourage his independence.
- Make sure your child understands all rules and the penalties for breaking them.
- Avoid power struggles with your child. Discipline is not a game in which there are winners and losers.
- Keep your sense of humor. It can work wonders with your child and help you keep your perspective about what is really important.
- Treat your child as you would your best friend—with respect, courtesy and love.

can be overcome if you watch TV with your child. Discuss what is happening. Ask such questions as "Are there really magic trolleys?" "Do you think all those cookies will give Cookie Monster cavities?" "Can people fly like that?" "How do you think that boy felt when the other boy took his toy truck?" "You've seen that toy in the store. Is it really that big and powerful?" By asking questions, you break the mesmerizing spell of TV and bring your child back to reality.

Sex Stereotyping Harms Girls and *Boys*

Do you dress your daughter in frilly dresses and continually admonish her not to play roughly or get dirty? Do you give your son blocks and a microscope, and your daughter dolls and a play stove? As your son approaches school age, do you talk about getting a home computer so he can work on it—though you've never worried about what your older daughter has missed because she hasn't had one at home? Do you tell your son that big boys don't cry? If so, you are sex-stereotyping your children.

Most American parents are still raising their children to hold so-called traditional views of the difference between boys and girls. It is no wonder, then, that studies show children start school with firm opinions of what is "women's work" and how "real men" behave. They learn these views at home, from friends and especially from TV, movies and magazines. While you can't protect your child from the sex stereotypes that abound outside your home, you can consider whether you are unconsciously teaching your child that boys are big, strong, active and brave, while girls are quiet, timid, delicate and charming; and that girls should like simple, pretty things to play with, while boys should favor big, complicated toys that they can build with, climb on or examine.

Such stereotyping will affect your child's success in school and in life. Studies have shown that girls are more successful in school and achieve more outside of school if they aren't socialized in the traditional way. Girls who are given trucks and blocks and chemistry sets are much more likely to do well in science and math than those who are given only dolls.

Girls who are taught to climb and jump and to try to win are more likely to try equally hard in school. Girls who are expected to compete and achieve are more likely to do so than those who are rewarded merely for being cute and obedient.

If you want your daughter to do her best in school and to achieve more in later life, treat her as a competent, independent and strong individual when she is young. Give her dolls *and* trucks, play kitchens *and* building blocks. Dress her appropriately for each situation. If she is going outside to play or to a friend's house, let her wear jeans so she can crawl around and hang from the monkey bars. Keep the frilly dresses for dress-up times and parties. While your daughter is young, introduce her to boys so that she will make friends of both sexes. And if you are going to buy a home computer, buy it for your daughter as well as your son. Encourage your daughter to use the home and school computers, to take computer classes and even to go to computer camp. Successful women are raised to be successful from birth.

The effect of sex stereotyping on boys' success in school is not as striking. Instead, sex-stereotyping your son is more likely to affect the way he relates to others. Boys who from childhood on are strongly socialized in the traditional male role are less likely to form warm and loving relationships with other people, and less likely to be able to express their feelings. Thus, while teaching your son to be macho rather than caring may not affect his school achievement, it may influence how well he makes friends and whether he has a happy marriage.

Raise your son and daughter to have the best attributes of both sexes.

Is Preschool Necessary?

As their child approaches the age of three, many parents begin to consider whether they should send him to preschool or nursery school. Twenty-five years ago, only about 11 percent of American children attended nursery school. By 1985 the number had increased to almost 40 percent and would probably have been even higher, except that many working parents find it impossible to fit preschool into their family's child-care arrangements.

According to many childhood educators, preschool can be valuable, though it isn't necessary for all children. In *Mis-education: Preschoolers at Risk,* David Elkind, a former president of the National Association for the Education of Young Children, wrote that preschool can increase "social experience by giving your child an opportunity to be with other adults and with a group of children of the same age. Because the range of toys and equipment is much greater than can be provided at home, the nursery school offers additional opportunities for the child to enhance a sense of autonomy, initiative and competence . . . [but it] is not essential for healthy development. If you have the time and energy to provide your child with a variety of social and educational experiences, you can also provide a rich early childhood program for your child at home."

For an only child, a child with few playmates in the neighborhood, a shy child or a child who lives in a small house or apartment, preschool is probably beneficial. Preschool allows children to learn to function without their parents, to relate to other caring adults, to deal with other children individually and in groups (especially to learn how to share), to make friends, to play with different toys, to show and tell about things that are important to them.

Studies have shown that preschool can have important, lifelong effects for certain groups of children: those with physical, mental or emotional disabilities, those growing up in poverty, those from non-English-speaking families and those from families with little experience concerning education. Federal law requires public schools to provide handicapped children with an appropriate education and other services from the time they are three years old. Such early intervention prepares many handicapped children for mainstream schooling. Federal programs such as Head Start as well as a number of experimental programs in public schools and private organizations have shown that preschool can remedy some of the disadvantages that poor and minority children may have. For example, in the Perry Preschool Project begun in Ypsilanti, Michigan, in 1962, black youngsters from low-income families who were given a high-quality preschool experience were still showing clear benefits at the age of nineteen. They did better in school and were more likely to graduate from high school and go on to college or get jobs than were similar children who didn't go to preschool. They were also less likely to commit crimes, have teenage pregnancies or need special education services while in school.

Though studies such as the Perry Preschool Project dramatically show how important it is for disadvantaged children to go to a good preschool, these findings shouldn't be translated to all children. Studies have not shown a similar impact on middle- or upper-class youngsters who already receive stimulation and teaching at home.

Unless your child needs special help, preschool is probably not crucial to his education. A good preschool program adds enjoyment and variety to the lives of three- and four-year olds, even to those from happy, well-educated and affluent homes. But almost 60 percent of all children don't go to preschool. If your child doesn't, he won't be at a disadvantage so long as you have provided him with what he needs at home.

Choosing a Preschool

If you decide to send your child to preschool, you may find that your community has only one, or that there are many from which to choose. Preschools are run by park districts, religious or community groups, local colleges or universities, groups of parents working together in cooperatives, and in some areas by public school districts. Before deciding where to send your child, learn what you can from friends and neighbors, visit the school(s) and talk to the school director.

No matter who runs a preschool, most fall into one of two categories—those that are academically oriented and those that aren't. The latter may call themselves "child-centered" or "enrichment-oriented." Whatever they call themselves, they are probably the kind of nursery school, centered on play, that has been popular for several decades. Today, though, many parents, in their desire to give their children a good start in life and a "leg up on the competition," are looking for preschools that begin formal academic training and may even teach children to read and write.

After many years of studying how children learn and develop, David Elkind strongly recommends against academic programs for preschool children. He believes that pressuring preschool-age children to read and to achieve academically can lead to learning problems and personality or emotional difficulties in later childhood and adolescence. According to Elkind, such difficulties might include the development of neuroses, compulsive behavior and phobias, or burning out and dropping out. So look for a preschool where children have a lot of time to play, to learn naturally through various projects, to explore, to try new things, to make new friends and to be successful at many activities, thus building their self-esteem.

A discussion of program goals with the head of the preschool as well as a look at the daily schedule will tell you what kind of a school it is. If the director talks about group instruction, tells you that the program is highly structured and points proudly to worksheets completed by the children, this is an academically oriented program. If instead you hear that the structure is loose, with large blocks of time devoted to "free play"—during which the children can move from activity to activity, undertaking or ignoring projects as they please—then this is a child-centered or enrichment-oriented program.

One type of program that doesn't fit either category is the Montessori school. These schools, which vary greatly in goals and operation, are based on the teachings of Maria Montessori, an educator who worked with young children in the slums of Italy early in this century. She designed school activities and materials to stimulate children's senses and to encourage them to explore and teach themselves. While these schools stress quiet activity, with children working alone or in small groups, rather than formal instruction, the children often learn to read and write at a very early age. The schools teach respect, responsibility and order with the children responsible for maintaining the classroom. Usually children are expected to scrub the tables and sweep the floors.

Whatever type of preschool you decide upon, check a number of factors besides philosophy and goals. Be sure that the teachers have the credentials required in your state. Even if they have the proper credentials and are trained in early childhood education, observe the classrooms to see if they are good at working with children, since a preschool is only as good as its teachers. Check the number of children in the school, and the number of teachers and helpers, too. A good ratio of students to staff is 5 or 6 to 1, but most preschools have a higher ratio. A higher ratio should not automatically exclude a preschool from your consideration, but weigh the ratio along with other factors, keeping in mind that a large class may be overwhelming to a shy three-year-old.

Check facilities and equipment. Do they appear safe? Are children closely monitored but allowed freedom at the same time? Is there a large and varied supply of toys? Many preschool rooms are divided into corners with toys for specialized activities; they may have a block corner, a housekeeping corner, a book center and a make-believe corner with clothing for dressing up. (David Elkind says that the first thing he looks for in a preschool is the block corner, since lots of big wooden blocks are a sign of a good preschool program.) Are there animals and plants for the children to watch? Is there an outside play area with safe and interesting equipment? Is there enough indoor space for the children to move around freely? Are snacks or other food nutritious and plentiful? Are books, easels and artwork on display? The answer should be

SKILLS KINDERGARTNERS NEED

World Book, Inc. recently surveyed more than three thousand kindergarten teachers to compile a list of skills they would like children to have upon entering kindergarten. Studying this list and seeing how many items your child has mastered will give you an idea of whether he is ready for kindergarten.

Teachers want students to have the following intellectual skills:

- Understanding size—what big and little, long and short mean.
- Being able to match objects according to size.
- Recognizing colors, shapes, numbers and letters; being able to name primary colors and basic geometric shapes.
- Being able to count to ten.
- Being able to recognize and print one's first name.
- Knowing one's address and parents' first and last names.
- Understanding words and stories.
- Being able to repeat a six- to eight-word sentence.
- Being able to identify the parts of the body.
- Understanding such opposites as up and down, in and out, hot and cold, back and front.
- Being able to follow simple directions.

❦ ❦ ❦

yes to all these questions. Are there workbooks and desks? Many early childhood educators would tell you to beware of any program with desks and workbooks or worksheets, since they believe that such tools of formal learning are not appropriate for preschool children.

Is Your Child Ready for Kindergarten?

Today some children have already spent two years in preschool or possibly five years in day care before they enter

- Being able to listen to a short story.

Teachers also want children to have the physical skills for:

- Running, jumping and hopping.
- Throwing a ball.
- Pasting.
- Cutting simple shapes.
- Clapping hands.
- Buttoning buttons and zipping zippers.
- Using crayons and pencils.
- Building with blocks.

Teachers look for these signs of children's social and emotional development:

- Being able to separate from their parents for a few hours.
- Using the toilet by themselves.
- Playing with other children.
- Talking easily.
- Working independently.
- Sharing with others.

school. For these children kindergarten is not as much of a leap as it is for children who have been at home all their preschool years. While kindergarten is still optional in some states, most American children do attend, starting approximately when they reach the age of five.

If your child lacks many of the skills suggested by kindergarten teachers, if his birthday falls near the cutoff date for school admission, or if he seems unusually shy or immature compared with others of his age, you may question whether he should start kindergarten at age five. Most experts will tell you that if you have doubts, the safest route is to wait. This is particularly true for boys, who tend to mature later than girls. Keeping children out of kindergarten for a year may mean that they will always be the oldest members of their class, but older children generally do better in school than younger ones. Today there is little or no stigma attached to delayed entry into school, but there continues to be one attached to repeating kindergarten or first grade. So, if it seems that school will be bewildering and frustrating for your five-year-old, keep him out for an extra year, and avoid a bad start to his school career.

Getting Ready for the First Day of School

"Even children who have attended two years of preschool or spent time at day-care centers and with babysitters are often nervous as that first day of kindergarten approaches," says Victoria Andrews, a former education specialist with the National PTA who taught kindergarten for ten years. "With advance planning, though, you can smooth your children's transition from preschooler to kindergartner."

Start the year before your child is scheduled to enter school. Contact the school secretary and ask to have your child's name put on the list for next year's kindergarten class. This will assure that you receive all mailings to the parents of prospective students. See if there are information packets for parents of kindergartners and if there is a school newsletter that you could receive. Find out whether kindergarten at your school is half-day or full-day; a number of schools are moving to full-day kindergarten, though most kindergarten students still attend only in the morning or afternoon. Also ask whether your child lives far enough away from school to take a school bus.

Learn from the school secretary or your local PTA president what school activities are open to prospective students and their families. For example, the PTA may sponsor a family fun festival or a spaghetti supper for members of the school community. If so, look over the school and show your child what fun school can be. Also, you may meet neighbors or some of your child's friends from preschool, which will help your child realize that not everyone at the new school will be a stranger. If you attend an open house, be sure to stop by the kindergarten room and say hello to the teacher. At the same time, it would be a good idea to join your local PTA and plan on attending a few meetings during the year to become acquainted with the school and its leaders.

Most schools have a kindergarten roundup, preregistration or open house, at which the teacher explains the kindergarten curriculum and lets the children get acquainted with their classroom. An apprehensive child is often greatly reassured by the sight of easels, gerbils and blocks. If possible, also show him the bathroom, the gym, the playground and, if he will be eating at school, the lunchroom.

Talk with your child frequently and positively about starting school. Read him books about school and tell him about your school days. If your child will be walking to school, walk with him often along the safest route. Practice crossing streets and looking for potential dangers, such as a bridge to cross. If your child will ride the bus, show him where he will get on and off, and talk to him about safe behavior on the bus. If he will not be bused, decide well before school starts whether you or someone else will walk or drive him to and from school, whether he will walk with an older sibling or neighbor, or whether he will walk alone after the first few days.

As summer nears its end, try to get your child into a schedule of going to bed earlier and getting up in time for school. Over several weeks, gradually make bedtime and wake-up time earlier and earlier until your child is into a routine. Also, according to Andrews, be sure that your child knows his name, address, phone number—including area code—and birth date, and that he can dress and undress himself alone. "And if you can help him learn to tie his shoes, his kindergarten teacher will be very grateful," says Andrews.

Also work on increasing the amount of independence and responsibility you allow your child. Praise him often for accomplishments, letting him know that you have confidence in his ability to take care of himself. While you will probably be somewhat apprehensive and even a little sad that he is old enough for such a big step as starting school, don't convey your worries or feelings to him. On the other hand, don't ignore or dismiss his fears. Instead, answer his questions as best you can and reassure him.

You may want to plan a shopping expedition a month or so before the start of school. Let your child pick out school clothes and items such as backpacks and lunch boxes. While you will want to label your child's clothes and belongings, for safety's sake don't put his name on his shirt, cap, jacket, backpack or anywhere else that it could be seen from the outside. Instead, you might want to write just his initials and phone number, so that items can be identified and returned but no one can learn his name or address from a carelessly discarded jacket or other item.

Be sure that your child knows other safety rules, such as how to cross streets, where to play, and what to do if approached by a stranger.

When the big day comes, walk or take your child to school. The kindergarten teacher may meet you at the door to escort him into the room. If he clings to you and cries, take your cue from the kindergarten teacher, since most have developed effective ways to get children interested in their new surroundings, and to let Mom or Dad leave. While it is heartbreaking to walk out as your child cries for you, try to do what the teacher advises so long as the teacher seems to be giving attention to your child's needs and isn't swamped with fifteen other crying children. *Then* go home or to work and shed a tear, or congratulate yourself on having made it this far as a parent. Be sure, though, to check with the teacher after school to see that your child settled down and joined the class soon after you left. If not, ask what the teacher advises to ease the separation in the future.

PTAs in Action

Many local PTAs have special programs for parents of preschoolers, including talks on child-rearing issues (for example, sibling rivalry and positive discipline), kindergarten readiness programs, school tours for parents and children, and support groups. Some communities have special preschool PTAs. Many elementary and junior high school PTAs also assist parents of preschoolers. Check with the PTA in your area to find out what it offers for parents of young children. These are examples of PTAs with programs for parents of preschoolers:

• The Wheaton-Warrenville Preschool PTA in suburban Chicago is one of the most active PTA groups. It holds many parent education programs as well as tours for parents and children to places of interest in the community. Every year the PTA plans a free community-wide project. One year the project was a three-part series on preventing sexual abuse, with workshops for parents and children aged three to six.

The PTA put together a newsletter filled with information on how parents can safeguard their young children from sexual abuse. It gathered more than forty handouts for parents to take home. Another year, when its community project was on safety, it scheduled parent workshops on such topics as home safety, water safety, bike safety, fire prevention and the safe use of electrical equipment. PTA leaders also assembled a list of community groups that provide classes or workshops of interest to parents of young children.

• In the neighboring communities of Glen Ellyn, Lombard and Villa Park, Illinois, the GLV Preschool PTA held a fair that introduced parents to thirty area preschools.

• The Richardson Preschool PTA in Richardson, Texas, hosts monthly potluck dinners at which experts talk about such topics as reducing stress, helping children handle fears and choosing books for preschoolers. Many of its activities involve both parents and children, like its "Moms and Munchkins," and "Dads and Kids" programs. It also runs a babysitting co-op and plans social activities such as bridge groups, softball games and craft demonstrations.

• The Stemmons Preschool PTA in Dallas, Texas, presented a "Safety with Animals" workshop. This PTA provides free vision and low-cost hearing tests for children in its community.

• The Hawthorne Preschool PTA in St. Joseph, Missouri, held a "Cooking with Preschoolers" program.

• The Bay Village Preschool PTA in Bay Village, Ohio, held a drug abuse prevention program for parents of preschoolers. It was entitled "Never Too Soon—Combating Chemical Dependency."

• The Medina Preschool PTA in Medina, Ohio, encouraged its local hospital to start a car seat safety program.

• The North Olmsted Preschool PTA in North Olmsted, Ohio, provides volunteers to work at a well-child clinic.

CHAPTER 3

Understanding Your Child's School

SUDDENLY ONE DAY you realize that there is a problem with your child and school. Maybe it's a problem with a subject—your daughter isn't learning to read as quickly as you and the teacher think she should. Maybe you disagree with a school rule. Maybe you think the teacher is not giving your child the help she needs, or maybe you just have an uneasy feeling that she isn't getting as good an education as you wish.

Once you recognize the existence of a problem, you are undoubtedly anxious to do something about it. But whom do you talk to? What can you expect from teachers and from your school? If you understand your child's school, you can answer these questions and are well on your way toward solving many school problems.

In many ways schools are like small communities, with officials, rules and traditions of their own. According to Robert Benton (the dean of education at the University of Wisconsin-Oshkosh, and formerly National PTA vice president for education and the chief state school officer for Iowa), "If parents want to get the best education for their children, they must first know the rules of the game and the respective players. Only then will they be able to become full partners in their children's education."

Start by learning where your child's school fits into the local, state and national education systems. First look at school funding and who makes the rules and policies for your school. You'll probably find that the source which provides most of the funding also wields most of the control since funding is usually tied to rules and regulations. On average nationally in 1988, 50 percent of local school funds came from state governments, 44 percent from local taxes and about 6 percent from the federal government. These percentages vary greatly from state to state. For example, in Hawaii more than 90 percent of school funds come from the state, in New Hampshire only about 7 percent.

State taxes are used to fund local schools because otherwise school districts in low-income areas would not be able to provide a good education for their students. Most states permit local school districts to spend additional money raised through local taxes. Therefore, some wealthy districts spend as much as $1,000 more per year per student than do nearby poor districts. Because of the state's role in equalizing educational opportunity, a cut in state funds usually hits low-income districts harder than rich ones.

Educating children is a state responsibility shared with local school districts. Some state governments exercise heavy control over local schools, while others exercise less, but all states establish the basic rules and the educational structure that regulate and shape your child's education. For example, states set school district boundaries, regulations under which school boards operate, the minimum number of days school must be in session each year, the ages at which children must start and be permitted to leave school, rules for teacher certification and high school graduation requirements. Some states also select textbooks that the schools must use, specify topics that must be taught and establish tests that students must pass in order to graduate or that teachers must pass in order to be employed. All states should challenge local school districts and individual schools to provide the best education possible, but the quality of educational leadership each state exerts varies greatly.

State rules are made by the state education department (headed by the chief state school officer, who is often called the state superintendent or education commissioner) and by the state legislature. Some states have effective superintendents and legislatures, and governors who are deeply committed to education. In other states, politics rather than educational needs is more likely to decide school funding and policies. A few months of attention to news about your state education department and legislature and a talk with your principal, PTA president or a school board member will give you an idea of the influence and control the state has over your local school district.

While the state government establishes general rules and goals for all schools in the state, the local school board sets most policies for local schools, approves the school budget and oversees operations. The board also hires the most important figure in your school district—the superintendent. Most school board members are elected, although in some areas they are appointed. Rarely are board members educators. Find out who your local school board members are, how they are selected and where they stand on important issues. Also, investigate ways to encourage capable individuals to run for your local board.

Good school board members bring to their position an interest in education, a concern for children and youth, a sound knowledge of their community and its wishes, a sense of fairness, a willingness to see all sides of issues, lots of common sense and patience. Good school boards recognize that it is their job to develop general policies and assure that the schools are well run, not to be actively involved in the day-to-day running of the schools. In most cases the board has the final authority in school finances and personnel matters, but a good board will not interfere in specific staffing matters, or try to dictate what kind of envelopes the district should buy. Instead, the daily operation of the schools is the responsibility of the superintendent—who is hired, and who can be fired, by the board.

Who's Who?

Knowing who is in charge is half the battle when solving any problem. Often when parents encounter a school problem, they think of only two people they can talk to—the classroom teacher and the principal—when there may well be another school official better suited to handling it. For this reason, you need to know the responsibilities of the main school officials. Since all schools and school districts differ, what is done by one official in one school may be the responsibility of another in a different school. You may want to make a list or chart of the key people, including titles and phone numbers. Your PTA may have already compiled such a list.

Superintendents oversee all the schools in their district, set the school schedule with board approval and coordinate everything that affects more than just one school. In your district, the superintendent probably has final responsibility for transportation, curriculum, dispersing the budget, hiring of personnel (including negotiating teacher or other union contracts) and selecting principals. In most districts, this is a very visible and powerful position. Depending on the size of the district, the superintendent may be assisted by a staff of assistant or deputy superintendents, financial officers, curriculum coordinators and transportation specialists, among others.

Over the last decades in many school districts, power and

decision-making authority have increasingly shifted from local schools and their principals to the central administration office and the superintendent and assistants. Decisions that were once made by principals are now often made by superintendents or other district office personnel, while decisions that were once made by teachers are now often made by principals. Currently, a movement is under way in some districts to decentralize power and return some of the decision-making authority to individual schools.

Principals are the key figures in local schools. Research has shown that a principal sets the tone for a school and, more than anyone else, influences how good an education that school offers. If a principal is a strong educational leader, students will probably learn more than if the principal is merely an administrator. So while principals must be good managers, they should also be active participants in curriculum decisions and be responsible for motivating, evaluating and rewarding teachers.

Principals oversee the spending of their school's budget, although the amount of their budget is set by the school board, which works in conjunction with the superintendent. Principals or their assistants schedule teachers, assign students to various classes and have the final say on discipline matters. The principal is the person to see if there is a problem with a teacher or with the school bus schedule.

Depending on the size of the school, there may be one or more *assistant principals,* who are in charge of such aspects of education as testing, discipline or curriculum. If you are ever uncertain about whom to talk to about a problem, call the school secretary in the principal's office. Another good source of information on who's who in your school is your PTA president, who also probably knows the real decision makers. In some schools, assistant principals have considerable power, while in others, most of the power rests with the principal.

Large schools, especially junior and senior high schools, often have *department heads*—usually experienced teachers who oversee and sometimes assign teachers in their department. Contact the math department head if you are concerned about the general math program in the school rather than with your child's grade in geometry. Don't confuse department heads with *curriculum coordinators*, *supervisors* or *specialists,* who are based in the central office, not in individual schools. You and your child may never see curriculum specialists or coordinators unless they participate in a parent information program sponsored by the PTA or the school, but they have a significant influence on what your child learns. They are not classroom teachers. As the resident experts in subjects such as math, English or the foreign languages, they help make decisions about the curriculum for all schools in the district.

Most high schools, many junior highs and even a few elementary schools have *guidance counselors*. Parents usually think of guidance counselors as staff members who help students figure out what college to attend, explain college financial aid, help fill out college applications and help students not going to college find jobs, but they may do much more. In many schools, counselors arrange students' class schedules, deal with discipline problems (for example, by contacting parents) and, as their name implies, counsel students on personal as well as educational problems.

Since high school students often have six or seven different teachers, it may be difficult for you to get an overall idea of how your child is doing. Therefore, you might set up an appointment with a guidance counselor or an assistant principal to discuss your child's educational progress and any general problems. You may need to contact the guidance counselor if you have questions about your child's schedule, if you are wondering whether she should consider college or if a problem has arisen in more than one of her classes. Sadly, most schools don't have enough guidance counselors—the national average is more than three hundred students per guidance counselor—so most counselors spend their time responding to problems and requests rather than actively seeking out students who need help.

A guidance counselor may suggest that you talk to the *school social worker* or a private social worker, or that your child see a private or *school psychologist* if there is a difficult or continuing problem. School social workers deal with students' educational and personal problems. Since the amount of time a school social worker can devote to any one student is limited, the social worker may refer you to a clinic or social worker in private practice if your child needs long-term help. Similarly, a school psychologist can provide only short-term counseling. In many schools, psychologists spend most of their time testing students to try to pinpoint the cause of learning or behavior problems. They have little time for traditional counseling. In any case, the school psychologist will refer you to an independent psychologist or psychiatrist if the problems are major. Many schools lack their own social workers or psychologists, and can only provide referrals.

If your child is injured on the playground or becomes ill during the school day, she may be sent to see the *school nurse* for first aid and an assessment of the need for further medical attention. The school nurse is also in charge of updating health records, including dates of immunization. Unfortunately, many schools have no nurse on the premises, leaving teachers or other staff members in charge of first aid. Find out whether your school has a nurse and, if not, who is responsible for health matters. If your child has a special medical condition such as diabetes, asthma or epilepsy, alert the school nurse or whoever handles first aid, and discuss emergency care.

Surprisingly, some schools don't have a *librarian* either. If your school does have one, get to know this person and be sure that your child does, too. A good school librarian can encourage students' love of reading and also suggest ways for parents to help their children with reading. When your school has an open house or back-to-school night, make it a point to visit the school library (often called the learning or media center) and meet the librarian.

If your child has special learning or physical problems or is gifted, you may become very familiar with the *reading specialist* or *reading teacher*, *special education teachers*, the *speech therapist* or *teachers for the gifted*. Reading specialists or reading teachers work with classroom teachers (particularly in the elementary grades), and individually or in groups with children who are having reading problems. In the same way, speech therapists work with students who have speech or language problems. Special education teachers may teach a group of students in a self-contained classroom or work one-on-one with individuals. *Teachers for the gifted and talented* usually work with students for a certain period of time each day or several days a week, although some teach full-time classes for gifted students.

A special staff member whom you definitely should get to know is the *school secretary*. Don't underestimate the role of the school secretary by assuming that she merely answers the phone and types memos. In most schools the secretary has her finger on the school's pulse. She is the keeper of information, a problem solver, a collector of lost items and a wonderful resource. If you don't know the person to see about a problem, ask the secretary. If you don't understand a school rule or the schedule, ask the secretary. If you are looking for child care for your school-age child, ask the school secretary if she knows any mothers who take care of children, or where other parents at the school find child care. If the secretary can't answer your questions, she can probably tell you who can. She can probably also find an extra copy of that important school memo that you misplaced, or help your child when she's lost her lunch money. For all these reasons, make a point of getting to know the school secretary and the other office staff. They can be great sources of formal and informal information about the school, teachers and classes.

The School Calendar and Day

The typical school calendar—nine months in school, with the summer off—was developed when America was a rural society and children were needed to work in the fields. Although the rationale for this schedule no longer exists, most schools have held on to it tenaciously. Only a few schools across the country have switched to a year-round schedule. If your school operates in this manner, students will probably attend classes the same amount of time—nine months—but their vacation months can occur during any time of the year. Supporters say that year-round schools are more efficient since school buildings don't sit empty for a quarter of the year. Such a schedule also helps alleviate the overcrowding that is a problem in some schools today. On the other hand, parents often say that year-round schools wreak havoc with family vacations and child care. A family with three children might have three different school vacation schedules. In addition, critics believe that students who have mostly midwinter vacations are shortchanged when compared with friends who have three months off during the summer. Whatever the merits of year-round schools, it seems unlikely that most school districts will move in that direction in the near future.

Although local school districts decide whether school will be year-round or not, states set the length of the school year. The average is 180 days. The length of the school day varies, too, though the average is six hours. In 1983 a Department of Education report, *A Nation at Risk*, called for lengthening both the school year and day, but many educators disagree. They believe that the key to improving schools is not spending more time, but rather using time better.

In his major study, entitled *A Place Called School: Prospects for the Future,* John Goodlad suggested that the amount of the school day actually spent in learning should be increased. His research showed that even a 10-percent increase in instructional time improves achievement. Goodlad found that teachers spend an average of 73 to 76 percent of class time actually teaching. The remainder of the time is allocated to housekeeping activities such as roll calls and lunch counts, collecting and returning assignments or listening to announcements over the loudspeaker. He recommends that teachers and schools increase the time spent in instruction and cut down on wasted time by finding more efficient ways to handle routine tasks.

Typically, school days for older children are divided into six or seven class periods that average forty to fifty minutes. One of these periods is usually lunch, and the rest are classes or study halls (some schools no longer have study halls). Students in the elementary grades spend all or most of their time with one teacher, who generally varies the amount of time spent on different subjects. Some elementary school students have different teachers for special subjects like art, music and physical education, while in other schools regular classroom teachers may teach these subjects, too.

In high school, students usually spend one class period on each subject, and they change classrooms and teachers after every period. This increases the amount of time spent in nonlearning activities, since students usually need a few minutes at the start and end of class to settle down or to gather their papers and books. Also, since students may have five or six different teachers each day, they don't develop the attachment to their teachers that elementary school students do. What students gain from this plan is access to teachers who have specialized in math, science or English, and who therefore have more expertise in the subject.

Either junior high or middle school usually follows elementary school. The grades included in elementary, junior high, middle and high schools differ from community to community. Some elementary schools include kindergarten through eighth grade, with high school covering ninth through twelfth grades. Some districts have grades K–6 in elementary school—with seventh and eighth, or seventh through ninth in junior high school. Other districts have replaced junior high school with middle school.

Middle schools, which cover grades 5–8 or 6–8 or even 6–9, are structured somewhat differently from junior highs. Junior highs usually follow the senior high pattern, with six or seven class periods a day and students moving from class to class and teacher to teacher. Middle schools, on the other hand, are designed to be a transition between elementary school and high school. Classes are organized into clusters of related subjects, so one teacher may handle a number of different classes. Thus, students only change classes and teachers three or four times a day.

What Is Taught?

All schools should have written goals and objectives. What translates these goals and objectives into classroom activities is the curriculum. Each subject and each grade should have a written plan detailing what will be taught. Check to see if your school has a parent/student handbook or curriculum outline giving an overview of your child's education.

The basic elementary school curriculum consists of language arts (reading, writing and spelling), math, social studies, science, music, art and physical education. Some elementary schools teach foreign languages, and an increasing number teach computer skills. In some districts, foreign languages aren't introduced until junior or middle school, or even high school. History, advanced math (such as algebra and geometry) and advanced science (including chemistry and physics) are some of the subjects that are usually added in middle, junior high or high school. Usually high school also offers more specialized classes, life-skills classes (many dealing with family living) and vocational or career-oriented classes.

Many educational reformers are critical of the typical elementary school reading program. Throughout much of American history, children were taught to read by the phonetic method—by sounding out the letters. Earlier in this century, though, some educators became convinced that children learned more rapidly and comprehended better if they were taught the whole word. This "look-say" method became the most popular one for teaching youngsters to read. However, starting in the 1950s, critics who complained that Johnny couldn't read often blamed Johnny's problems on the fact that he wasn't taught phonics. Today most elementary educators agree that students should be taught phonics, but they claim that too much concentration on phonics can make reading extremely boring and prevent students from comprehending what they are reading. Most educators believe that students should get a good grounding in phonics initially, but that around the end of the second grade, they should move on to concentrating on improving their skills and increasing comprehension, unless they are having trouble.

By the time students get to high school and sometimes even before, many are either consciously or unconsciously heading along one of three paths, or tracks. The brightest, college-bound students are directed along an academic track, taking classes such as four years of English, advanced math and science, and probably a foreign language. Other students are encouraged to take a general education track, with less difficult courses—maybe only three years of English plus life-skills and work-related electives. A third group of students is directed along a strictly vocational path, taking fewer academic subjects and spending part of the time preparing for jobs such as typist or machine operator.

Tracking is highly controversial today, although most

parents like it. The parents of a college-bound student are happy that their child is getting the courses required for college admission, while the parents of a student entering the work force right after high school think that she is being well prepared for employment. Many educational reformers, though, don't like the tracking system because they think it cheats many students in the general education and vocational tracks out of a really good education. It prevents them from changing their mind about what to do after high school, since they won't have the courses necessary for college admission. Also, these critics charge that vocational education in most high schools is so out-of-date that it is preparing students for nearly obsolete industrial and clerical jobs. For example, students are being trained as typists rather than as word processors. Many business and industry leaders dislike tracking, too, charging that the attention paid to training for specific jobs should be spent teaching students how to read, write and think. These business leaders say that they can teach high school graduates to do specific jobs, but they can't give them the academic training that was missing in school.

Many educators recommend the elimination of all forms of tracking. John Goodlad, a professor of education at UCLA and one of the nation's leading authorities, has called for schools to provide a core curriculum for all students. Goodlad says that schools today are like two worlds—the academic and the vocational—with a disproportionately high percentage of minority and poor children being relegated to the vocational track. He cites research that found lower self-esteem, more discipline problems and higher dropout and delinquency rates in the lower tracks. He also studied non-tracked classes and found that teachers can motivate the slower students as well as challenge the brightest ones. For these reasons, Goodlad has called for the end of tracking in the elementary through high schools, and for assigning students to classes and ability groups at random.

Ernest Boyer, president of the Carnegie Foundation for the Advancement of Teaching, agrees. "Putting students into boxes can no longer be defended," he wrote in *High School*. "To call some students 'academic' and others 'nonacademic' has a powerful and, in some instances, devastating impact. . . . Students are divided between those who think and those who work, when, in fact, life for all of us is a blend of both. . . . Therefore, we recommend that the current three-track system . . . be abolished. It should be replaced by a single-track program—one that provides a core education for all students plus a pattern of electives, keeping options open for both work and further education."

If, as you begin to understand your school and become more involved in your child's education, you find that tracking is used, check with the guidance counselor to see which track your child is on. Even if she is on an academic track, see if there are vocational or life-skills courses that she should take to supplement the academics. If she is on a general or vocational track, insist that she take the appropriate academic classes to prepare her either for work or college. If you find that tracking is a problem in your school, ask your PTA president to call a meeting about it, since educated and alert parents can prevent their children from being shortchanged as well as pressure the school to end this system.

The Discipline Code

Even though you hope that your child will never get into trouble, you need to know what the school rules say about discipline problems and procedures. Most schools carefully spell out various infractions and the possible punishments. Your school's discipline code may be in the parent/student handbook. If it isn't, ask the school secretary for a copy of the policy, read it carefully and explain it to your child.

If your school doesn't have a written discipline policy,

your PTA may suggest that a written behavior code for students be drawn up. Or if the existing policy is vague, unclear or otherwise unsatisfactory, your PTA may push for it to be revised. Studies have shown that the most effective school rules and discipline policies are those which students and parents have helped set and which encourage students to be self-disciplined. Poorly developed and understood rules, and those that are only sporadically or unevenly enforced increase discipline problems. So suggest to your PTA or principal that students be involved in efforts to strengthen the discipline code or to increase compliance with it.

When looking at a school discipline policy, find out what behavior will lead to disciplinary action and how discipline will be handled. In general, schools have a system of increasingly severe responses, which may begin with a verbal followed by a written warning, then move on to in-school detention (such as having to stay after school for a certain length of time), suspension for one or more days, and finally expulsion from school for serious misconduct. Parents should be notified promptly of all disciplinary actions taken against their children.

At one time many schools were quick to suspend or expel students, but court decisions have affirmed certain student rights, such as the right to due process and to present a defense. Still, the U.S. Department of Education's Office for Civil Rights estimated that there were nearly 2 million students suspended from schools in 1986. It is possible that at some time your child or the child of a friend might face suspension. For this reason you will want to read carefully what the discipline code says about such punishment. If the code is not clear, ask for additional information.

Also check your school's policy on corporal punishment—paddling, slapping and other physical measures. A few states and some large school districts have outlawed corporal punishment, but it is still used in many American schools.

The U.S. Department of Education's Office for Civil Rights estimated that corporal punishment was used on nearly 1.1 million American public school students in 1986.

"The National PTA opposes the use of physical punishment for any reason in our schools," states Joan Ball, a PTA leader from Spring Valley, New York, who has helped lead the fight against corporal punishment for the last twenty years. "The PTA and other groups opposing corporal punishment believe that physical abuse never achieves what it is supposed to do—that it does not teach students self-discipline and thus is not effective. It is also demeaning and very destructive to students' self-esteem. This is particularly regrettable since many children act up in school because they lack self-esteem and because they know of no other way of expressing their anger and frustration except through physical violence. Physical punishment sets a bad example because it shows students that physical might makes right." The use of corporal punishment may also be biased, since boys are most often the victims of physical punishment, as are minority students.

The discipline children learn at home is the foundation for their behavior at school, so you should always view a school discipline problem as a home problem, too. If your child's teacher or principal reports a discipline problem, talk with this individual as well as your child. Don't immediately jump to your child's defense, but also don't overreact and punish her until you have learned the whole story. Everyone concerned should work out a solution together that will prevent further misbehavior.

If there are school rules that you oppose, work through your PTA to change them. Remember that schools function well only when parents support the schools' rules, so let your child know that you expect her to abide by them. As in so many other cases, be sure that you set a good example. Don't violate school rules, for example, by writing phony excuses when your child skips class or by covering for her when she breaks rules. And, children notice if you disobey speed limits or brag about how you cheat on your income tax, or if you talk about how you used to get away with skipping school.

Spotting a Good Teacher

Some students will learn no matter what kind of teachers they have, but for many students, good teachers make the difference between a mediocre education and an excellent one. Undoubtedly, one of your chief concerns is whether your school has good teachers.

Think about the teachers you had in school—the ones you liked and those you didn't. Did some manage to involve you in the subject they were teaching and make you want to learn? Did certain ones make you feel that you could ask them anything you wanted about their subject? Did the best teachers make you think and participate in class rather than allow you to hide behind the student sitting in front of you and sneak peeks at the clock on the wall to see how much time was left in the period? Were some teachers so exciting that you looked forward to their classes? Did a few teachers even talk *with* students rather than lecture *at* them day after day? Did you notice that in some classes time flew by because you were busy every minute rather than playing with your pencil and daydreaming while waiting for the class to start, or the teacher to pass out and collect homework? Did the best teachers treat all students as part of the class rather than ignore the slow students, because they were going to do poorly, and the smart ones, because they could take care of themselves? If you can answer yes to many of these questions, then you are remembering effective teachers—those who helped you learn the most.

While these teachers had different styles, personalities and teaching methods, didn't they share certain characteristics?

TEN THINGS PARENTS WISH TEACHERS WOULD DO

1. **Build students' self-esteem** by using praise generously, and avoiding ridicule and negative public criticism.
2. **Get to know each child's needs,** interests and special talents, as well as the way each child learns best.
3. **Communicate often and openly with parents,** contacting them early on about academic or behavioral problems and being candid rather than defensive when discussing these problems.
4. **Regularly assign homework** that helps children learn, and advise parents how they can work with their children on this homework.
5. **Set high academic standards,** expecting all students to learn and helping them to do so.
6. **Care about children,** since children learn best when taught by warm, friendly, caring and enthusiastic teachers.
7. **Treat all children fairly** and not play favorites.
8. **Enforce a positive discipline code** based on clear and fair rules that are established at the beginning of each school year; reinforce positive behavior rather than punish negative behavior.
9. **Vary teaching methods** and make learning fun.
10. **Encourage parent participation** by reaching out to involve parents in their children's education, showing them how they can help their children at home and remembering that parents want to work with teachers to help their children do their best.

Good teachers never write off any student. They don't have one set of standards for good students and lower standards for others. They know that students learn at different rates—some are faster than others, some need more help than others—but they are convinced that all students can learn, and that it is their job to see that all students do. Having high expectations for all students and helping them fulfill their potential is the most important thing teachers can do, because those students who are expected to do well usually succeed, while those who are expected to fail usually do so.

The importance of praise as a motivator can't be overestimated either. Too often teachers, like parents, take for granted good behavior or success, commenting only on misbehavior or failure. Successful teachers continually praise and reward their students. They set up situations in which students can succeed. However, John Goodlad's studies, reported in *A Place Called School,* found that most teachers rarely praise students. For this reason it is doubly important for parents to praise their children for jobs well done at school.

Good teachers establish a warm and caring atmosphere in their classes. Sadly, though, Goodlad's studies found that there was a feeling of restraint and neutrality in most classrooms—Goodlad characterized them as "flat." He found little student-teacher conflict, but little feeling of warmth, either, in the classrooms he studied. For some reason, warmth and enthusiasm for the subjects taught often go together. Thus, good teachers can make a subject come alive whether it is chemistry, English literature or the multiplication tables, and they make all students feel appreciated and cared about.

Good teachers use class time well. They keep students at work and the class moving along. Part of the way they do this is by establishing clear rules and procedures at the start of the year, and then maintaining those rules. For each lesson they explain what they intend to do, follow through step-by-step, and sum up when they are finished. They give clear instructions and quick feedback, correct errors and show students that they are being listened to. While good teachers are well organized, they don't overmanage their classes. They encourage students to contribute and are willing to move the class in a new direction if it seems more understandable and interesting to the students.

What good teachers don't do is spend forty-five minutes of a fifty-minute period lecturing to their students. Of course there are times when teachers must lecture or explain something in detail, but as much as possible good teachers use other techniques besides lectures, because they know that students learn better when they are actively involved rather than passively listening and taking notes.

Keep these characteristics of good teachers in mind when you meet your child's teacher and if you observe a class. Remember that teachers may either be dressed for success or wearing jeans; they may or may not look like the teachers you had when you went to school; they may have unusual teaching styles; but all good ones motivate and reward students, and involve students actively in their education.

Good teachers should be rewarded. You personally can help reward your child's teacher by recognizing what a hard job it is to be a teacher. Have you ever spent the day trying to interest and teach 25 seven-year-olds? Be sure to tell your child's teachers how much you appreciate their efforts. Thank them warmly and sincerely. Send them personal notes when they do something special for your child or even just to tell them how pleased you are with the way the year is going. Send the principal a copy of any special thank-you notes, and drop the principal or department head a note to report outstanding teachers or those who go out of their way to help students. And support efforts to reward teachers financially as well. Keep your eye on teacher salaries in your local school budget, and encourage schools to work to improve teachers' salaries and working conditions.

If Your Child Gets a Lemon

If your school is good, most teachers will probably be good, too, and a few may even be outstanding. But Bill Honig, state superintendent of public instruction in California, has estimated that between 5 to 10 percent of all teachers are incompetent. No one knows how many others are mediocre or not as good as they could be. So what can you do if your child gets one or, worse yet, a series of bad teachers? There may not be much you can do, but this shouldn't deter you from trying to do something about the situation.

You may begin to be concerned about a teacher because your child claims the teacher picks on and belittles her. Try to talk to your child and get all the specific information that you can. While you shouldn't automatically take everything your child says as gospel, don't dismiss her complaints either. Instead, listen and try to find out if there was a misunderstanding, if there was a single incident that upset your child, or if there is a continuing problem. Has your child always gotten along with teachers, or has she often had problems with them? Is she overly dramatic? Does she often feel picked on? Is she the kind of child who is likely to talk back to teachers or be disruptive in class? You know your child better than anyone else, so you should have a good idea of how real the problem with her teacher is.

Maybe there is no specific problem or complaint from your child, but you notice that she never has homework in one class and never brings home papers or studies for exams either. When you ask about this class, she may say that it is really boring because the teacher wastes time or is often "out of it." In this case, make it a point to get to know the teacher. Does this individual seem disorganized, uncertain and vague? Keep a close eye on that class, and watch what your child says and brings home. If after a month or so your child says that the teacher is still trying to get organized, or if she comments that classes are a total waste, you may well ask yourself, "What should I do?" If you know parents of other students in the class, you might ask them about their children's perceptions.

If there is a particular incident or general concern you

want to discuss, you may decide to ask for a formal meeting with the teacher. This is where you should always start if there is a classroom problem. Even if you believe that the problem is with the teacher, don't go directly to the principal. You may well end up going to the principal, but you will get a much better reception if you first try to work out the problem with the teacher. Besides, this meeting may bring about a solution, or maybe you'll conclude that your child was wrong.

Call the teacher and ask for a conference. If there is a specific incident, such as a time when your child thought the teacher humiliated her in front of the class, be prepared to discuss this incident calmly, and to listen carefully to the teacher's explanation. Don't go in looking for a fight. Rather, view the meeting as a time to learn what happened. Try to be as objective as possible, and see if you and the teacher can solve the problem.

It is more difficult to deal with a general problem. If your child says she is not learning anything in a class because the teacher is "absolutely awful," consider approaching the teacher and saying that your child has always liked and done well in math, but that this year she seems to be lost, that she doesn't understand what is expected and therefore doesn't feel that she is making any progress. Don't tell the teacher that she isn't doing her job. Instead, outline the problem and see if you can work out a solution that will provide more of whatever your child needs. Thus you might tell a teacher who seems to be chronically disorganized that your child has always needed a lot of structure, direction and feedback—can the two of you figure out a way to provide these? Maybe in talking to you the teacher will realize some of her shortcomings and begin to think of ways to strengthen her teaching methods.

If you are still concerned after the conference, you will have to decide what, if anything, to do next. If you elect to talk to a superior, call the school secretary and ask if it is appropriate to meet with the principal or if there is another administrator with whom you should schedule an appointment. Most likely you will be told to make an appointment with the principal. Many parents are afraid to go over a teacher's head because they fear that the teacher will take it out on their child. Though some might do this, most won't. Still, you should realize that going to a higher level will probably mean that you will never be able to develop a close working relationship with that teacher. Maybe you don't care because you think the teacher is so bad that such a relationship isn't possible. However, consider carefully how important the problem is before seeking out the principal.

As part of your preparation for meeting with the principal, check over all the papers your child has brought home from that class. Consider whether other parents share your concern. If so, ask one or two to accompany you, but don't arrive with a thirty-person delegation. Be aware that the principal will probably ask the teacher to attend the conference. Whether you go alone or with a few other parents, be sure to begin by telling the principal that despite a previous discussion with the teacher involved, you are still concerned and would like to discuss the matter further. Review the problem calmly. Don't make sweeping judgments, for example, saying that the teacher is unfit to teach. The principal can draw conclusions on the basis of prior knowledge of the teacher, in addition to your carefully presented information. Rather than blaming the teacher, present the problem and ask if the discussion can center on what can be done to improve the situation.

If you can keep the conversation from degenerating into accusations—"the teacher did such and such" and "your daughter did this or that"—you will increase the chances of working out a solution, since you won't make the principal feel the need to defend the teacher. In fact, if you state the case carefully, you may find that the principal has been aware of the teacher's problems for a while and welcomes the opportunity to help this individual. For example, the principal may offer to work with the teacher on organizing class time. Or maybe the principal will suggest ways in which the teacher can work more effectively with your child. Listen carefully to any suggestions the principal makes and see if you can add your own ideas for moving the teacher in a productive direction. If the principal suggests something that you think has merit, warmly endorse it and offer to do everything in your power to make it work. Before you leave the meeting, sum up what was agreed upon and ask for a follow-up meeting to review progress in a month or two.

If you receive no satisfaction or workable suggestions from your meeting with the principal, you are in a difficult situation. You can appeal the principal's decision to the superintendent and ultimately to the school board, but while there is a tendency for principals to back their teachers, there is an even greater likelihood that superintendents will back their principals, since most superintendents hate to overrule the administrator closest to the problem. So you will have to decide once again whether the matter is worth pursuing. Ask yourself: Is my child suffering emotionally or academically? Can I help my child in other ways? For example, would a math tutor or a summer school algebra course fill in what the teacher isn't providing? Is the school year so close to being over that my child can ride out the situation?

If there is a problem that goes beyond this one teacher, such as a generally low level of teaching, you may want to pursue the matter even if you can't change anything in this class. Also, you may want to ask your PTA president to schedule one or more meetings on what makes effective teachers and what can be done to improve teaching in your school. The PTA may also want to look into the way teachers are evaluated and to call for more effective teacher evaluations, which might be combined with higher pay. But don't expect your PTA to try to oust a teacher.

Be aware that even if you decide to fight your way up the administrative ladder and to do everything possible to solve the problem with a teacher, many problems aren't easily solved. Even if you think that the teacher is incompetent and should be fired—and other parents agree with you—you probably won't succeed if the teacher is tenured. The California superintendent of public instruction recently estimated that it can take several years and as much as $70,000 to fire a tenured teacher in his state. Most schools aren't willing to undertake such a fight unless the situation is intolerable.

You may think that a better route is to try to get your child transferred to another class. Again, this is hard to do. While parents can often influence class assignments at the start of the year, principals are rarely willing to transfer students in midyear because of problems with a teacher. Still, it may be worth asking for a transfer if there is no other way out.

Your best bet for improvement is to come to an agreement with the teacher, or the teacher and the principal. You may well be able to accomplish this, because most teachers genuinely want to do their best. They will try to improve their teaching or to deal more fairly with an individual student. Likewise, principals want their teachers to do a good job, and they want happy, satisfied parents, so principals will usually try to work out a solution acceptable to both. If you help the principal, and let the teacher save face in the process, you may find that the situation can be improved enough for your child and you to survive the year.

The School Budget

If you are going to understand your child's school, you've got to understand its budget, because it reflects in concrete terms your school district's goals and priorities, and influences the quality of education. Understanding your school budget may appear to be an overwhelming job, particularly if you have a hard time figuring out your own family budget, but it can be done if you are willing to do some studying. An excellent resource is Rhoda Dersh's book, *School Budget: It's Your Money,* which will provide you with a general understanding of your school district's budget-making process without requiring that you become an expert in the field. Much of the next section is based on Dersh's work.

As a first step to understanding the budget, contact your local PTA president, superintendent or a school board member. Ask if the PTA president, a PTA member who monitors the budget or a school administrator can give you a quick overview. If you can't get the information you need from one of these sources, consider getting together with several other parents to gather information and analyze the budget. In this way you'll divide up the work and, as a member of a group of concerned citizens, you'll have a much greater influence on budget decisions. Next, call your superintendent's office and tell the secretary that you are a citizen (don't identify yourself as Susie Smith's mother) and would like: (1) a copy of the current budget, (2) the proposed budget for next year if it has already been developed, (3) the district's current and long-range educational plans, and any statements of goals and (4) the district's budget calendar (the schedule for budget hearings and consideration). Plan to attend the annual public hearing. Later, if you and your group decide to dig into the budget further, you may want other information, such as the budgets for previous years, year-end reports of actual expenses and revenue for the previous two years, and budget policies and guidelines.

The secretary may seem surprised as you go through this list, since few people make such detailed requests, but remember that you are entitled to this information. Then ask the secretary if you can obtain copies of this material. If you are told that the material is not available, ask with whom you need to make an appointment to get the information.

If the school district conducts its budget process in an open and orderly manner, the secretary will tell you that all the information you wish is on file in one place and that you can get copies either free or for the cost of duplication. Some schools are not orderly or willing to provide information, in which case you may have to work harder to get it. Remember, though, most states have "freedom of information" or "right to know" laws that allow citizens to see public records. Since all these documents fall under that category, you should be able to get the information you need if you are persistent.

You may also want to obtain budget-related information from your state education department. Especially useful is an annual financial statistical report on schools in the state. Most states have such a report, which lists revenue and spending for all districts in the state as well as other information, such as per pupil expenditure rates and teacher/student ratios.

Once you get your material, give it a quick review. What is the annual expenditure? The total revenue? What percent comes from local taxes, from the state and federal governments? Since most current budgets include information about the previous year's budget, see how the budget has increased or decreased. If you have asked for budgets from earlier years, you can get a much better picture of changes. If there has been a large change, in which areas did it come? Did a local property tax increase expand the budget? Have state funds increased? Have federal funds decreased markedly?

As you glance through the budget the first time, notice whether it seems to be well prepared. Is it laid out in an orderly and understandable manner? Does it include the basic four features of a well-prepared budget: (1) information on expected revenue, (2) anticipated spending or expenditures, (3) the outline of the general educational plan for the district and (4) a listing of current priorities? At the minimum, a budget should have revenue and expenditure information, but it is more informative if the connections are drawn between the dollars and the education plan and priorities.

As you go through the budget a second time, notice funding for areas that are of particular importance to your child. If she is in special education or gifted programs, has funding increased, decreased or stayed about the same over the last two years? Are there any programs for which funding has been drastically slashed or increased? For example, you may see that recent budget cuts have wiped out the art program, or that funds have been increased for team sports while those for physical education have been cut. Note the percentage increase in the overall budget, and the percentage change in specific areas. Have teachers' salaries increased more or less rapidly than other areas? If the total budget has increased 7 percent over the last year, you might find, for example, that teachers' salaries have increased by 11 percent, while transportation has increased by 25 percent and classroom materials by only 2 percent. Such variations will give you an idea of questions you may want to ask. Also see if the budget spells out how much is spent per student. If it doesn't, you can calculate this by dividing the total budget expenditure by the number of students.

You should also learn about the budget-making process. How much public, especially parent, input is allowed? Most schools have at least one public hearing on their budget, but some districts welcome community input throughout the budget-making process, and they provide numerous opportunities for community discussion. These districts realize that citizens are more supportive of budgets that they have helped to make.

After you've read through the budget, you may put it in a file and make a mental note to watch for future budget information sent home from the school or published in the local newspaper. Or you may want to delve more deeply into the budget and its ramifications for the children in your community. If you decide to look into the budget in depth, you may want to compare per pupil spending in your district to spending in other districts near you or across the state and nation, or to group expenditures into major categories and chart them to see where school money goes. You may want to check how well the district links dollars to the goals and priorities it has established. You may also want to see how well the budget is adhered to. The school board can make transfers from one area to another once the budget has passed, and a comparison of a recent budget and the year-end summary of expenses can show if transfers are a common occurrence.

Studying the budget in depth will be much easier if you work with others. A group is essential, too, if you decide to try to change budget priorities or procedures. "One parent working alone is much less effective than a group," advises Millie Waterman, a National PTA leader from Mentor, Ohio, who has spent many years studying school budgets. "Working through your PTA gives you help from other parents and from educators who already have knowledge about budgets, provides others to testify along with you at public hearings or otherwise back you up, and allows the slow building up of parent expertise and involvement. In this way you guarantee that others will continue to keep an eye on the budget if you should move away or become less involved in the schools once your children graduate."

PTAs in Action

Most PTAs hold workshops or parent education meetings to explain how their schools operate and to provide information about getting assistance with school problems. Thousands of PTAs have also established teacher recognition programs.

Many hold ceremonies to honor teachers, often during the National PTA's Teacher Appreciation Week, the first full week in May. Your PTA might want to consider adapting one of the following programs to help parents understand their school, or to honor teachers:

- The Scottsville Elementary School PTA in Scottsville, Pennsylvania, held "Curriculum Workshops" to show parents what their children were studying at school. The workshops, which provided parents with hands-on activities, included a computer lab and a discussion of the art program.
- The White Oak PTA in White Oak, Pennsylvania, holds an annual meeting that gives parents an overview of the school district and curriculum.
- The Benfield Elementary PTA in Severna Park, Maryland, wanted parents to understand the curriculum and learn what their children were doing every day in school, so it offered an eight-week program that focused on topics such as the science curriculum, foreign languages, and reading and writing instruction.
- The Key Elementary PTA in Arlington, Texas, scheduled a parent workshop entitled "Discipline Is the Key," which stressed the ways parents can foster self-discipline.
- The Thomas Jefferson Elementary PTA in Yorktown Heights, New York, has made one of its goals the involvement of parents in the budget-making process. To get parents interested and informed, PTA leaders attached to the PTA newsletter a "Budget Bulletin," providing information on the proposed budget and possible cuts, budget meetings and ways parents can give their input on the budget. Many parents who never bothered to learn about the school budget have become interested, and these budget-monitoring activities have helped the PTA develop a close working relationship with the superintendent and school board.
- When a new superintendent of schools was hired in Trumbull, Connecticut, Trumbull PTA Council leaders pre-

sented him with their concerns. Recognizing that money was the key to many of those concerns, the superintendent formed a budget committee of PTA members representing all the schools, and including special education students, in the district. The committee met weekly to discuss the budget and educational priorities. It held a series of PTA-sponsored "Coffees with the Superintendent" at each school to explain the budget and win community support for continuing existing educational services and reestablishing many that had been cut in recent years. After the budget was passed, the committee continued to meet to discuss major policy decisions, prepare long-range planning and get ready for the next year's budget.

• Since 1974, the Chicago Region PTA has administered the Kate Maremont Foundation Awards to honor outstanding teachers. Each year PTAs, teachers, principals, parents and students nominate outstanding teachers for this award, which is supported by the nonprofit Maremont Foundation. A PTA committee selects the top two teachers plus eight runners-up, presenting them with a cash award and plaques in a ceremony widely covered by Chicago-area media. The Chicago Board of Education supports the program. On the tenth anniversary of the awards, the Board found that almost all the teachers honored in the previous years were still teaching in the same district.

• The Beacon Hill PTA in Kelso, Washington, decided to honor its teachers in a different way for each day of Teacher Appreciation Week. On Monday, members put up a special bulletin board with the slogan "Our Teachers Are Special." On Tuesday, they placed a large cake in the teachers' lounge that was topped with the words "Hurray for Teachers!" On Wednesday, two parents dressed in nurses' uniforms handed out Teachers' First Aid Kits, containing items spelling out "teacher"—*t*issues, *e*raser, *a*spirin, *c*andy, *h*ot chocolate, *e*arplugs and *r*uler. On Thursday, donuts were served in the teachers' lounge, and a sign saying WE APPRECIATE OUR

TEACHERS was hung at the school entrance. On Friday, each teacher was presented with a special card.

• The Ocean Beach PTA in San Diego, California, asked parents to send thank-you notes to their teachers, and it sent a thank-you note from the PTA to each teacher.

• The Yankee Ridge PTA in Urbana, Illinois, encouraged children to write thank-you notes to their teachers. The notes were read at a special teacher appreciation luncheon that the PTA held.

• PTA members from Lincoln Junior High PTA in Morton Grove, Illinois, dressed in clown suits and presented apples to teachers during Teacher Appreciation Week. The activity was videotaped and shown to the school board to demonstrate parent and community support for teachers.

• In Piedmont, South Carolina, ninety local PTA units put up a billboard, prepared radio and TV public service announcements, wrote a TV editorial and arranged for business marquees to salute teachers.

• The R. O. Nelson PTA in Newport News, Virginia, gathered items from businesses in its community to present to teachers. Among the donated items were free haircuts and manicures, discount tickets to nearby Williamsburg and a free week at a health spa.

• Thousands of other PTAs provided sweet rolls, muffins, apple pies and a variety of other items to salute teachers. Still others provided or arranged for such services as having all the teachers' cars washed or taking over teachers' hall or lunchroom duty for a day or week. Many PTAs extend their recognition to cover all school staff. The Southport Elementary PTA in Indianapolis, Indiana, held a Staff Appreciation Week, during which food treats were provided for all staff, VIP buttons were distributed and the teachers' lounge, cafeteria and custodian's room were decorated.

CHAPTER

4

How Is My Child Doing?

THE SCHOOL YEAR has been under way for a month. You and your child are back in the routine of making lunches, doing homework and getting off in time in the morning. Now you have a few minutes to wonder: how is my child doing this year? Is everything going well? Are there any problems to worry about?

"There are both formal and informal ways to tell how your child is doing in school," says Ann Lynch of Las Vegas, Nevada, the 1989 National PTA nominee for president. "The most important gauge of the year's progress is probably your child's attitude. Does he talk happily about school? Does he tell you about the teachers and students and what he is doing during the day?

"Talking about school and relating the day's events are especially important for young children," Lynch continues. Children who like kindergarten, and first and second grades are usually bubbling over when they come home. They're anxious to tell you about their successes—"I was the only one in the whole class who could tie my shoes"—and to seek comfort for their failures—"I tried and I tried but couldn't figure out how to make an *s*"—and to show you their artwork and special projects.

"If there is one piece of advice I would give parents, it would be to devote the first twenty minutes that they see their child after school to talking to him about his day," Lynch adds. "You will probably learn more in those twenty minutes than from spending an hour trying to question him after dinner. I know that with so many two-career and single-parent families, many parents are tired, harried and hungry when they get home or when they pick their child up from his after-school baby-sitter, but if you can put aside the worries of the day and sit down right away with your child, you will find out a remarkable amount about how he is doing in school as well as what he is worried about or proud of."

By listening carefully to what your child does and does not say, asking questions and showing that you are interested, you can stay involved in what he is doing in school. Otherwise, you will have no idea what your child is learning and how he spends his school days. Pay particular attention to comments about teachers. Is Mrs. M. "really great"? Does the child seem scared of Mr. Jones? Do you hear comments like "She doesn't listen to me" or "He never answers my questions. I don't think he likes me"? Your interest shows your child that you value his education as well as care for him. You can also pick up early signs of problems if your child's comments are always negative or if they sound frustrated and confused.

While young children are usually anxious to talk about school, older ones, preteens and teens often aren't. Questions about what they did that day may be answered with a curt "Nothing." Don't be discouraged. Your child may just be in an uncommunicative phase. Try not to ask general questions like "How was your day?" or "What did you do in school?" Instead ask specific questions about friends and after-school activities, or the homework he was working on last night. If, over a period of time, your teen continually refuses to talk about school, you may have reason to be concerned. In that case, consider talking to his teacher.

Along with listening to what your child says, notice how eager he is to go to school. Most children like school because they see their friends and enjoy learning about new things. Some, however, dislike school or are hesitant about attending. Shy young children and those who are particularly dependent on their parents may have a hard time at the start of the school year. If this happens with your child, talk to his teacher. Teachers are old hands at dealing with beginning-of-school problems. As the routine becomes established, the fear should lessen and then disappear.

If your child continues to cry in the morning, complains day after day of stomachaches or headaches, or seems nervous and upset about going to school, you need to look for more help. Talk to the teacher again or to the school nurse. See if there is a school counselor who could offer suggestions. Perhaps you will want to check with your doctor. Most important, try to find out what is bothering your child. Is there a problem with other children: a schoolyard bully or someone on the school bus; a problem understanding a school rule, such as how to get permission to go to the restroom; a problem with the teacher; a physical problem, such as not being able to see the board clearly; or a problem doing schoolwork?

While you don't want to overreact, don't let a bad situation drag on, either. Instead, try to find out what is wrong and how it can be fixed. Children who are afraid of something, or who for some reason don't like school, usually have trouble learning. They may not do well because they dislike school, or they may dislike school because they already realize they are not doing well. Thus, their attitude toward school may give you an early indication that problems exist.

While some problems in the early years just fade away, others don't. For example, children who don't like school will often be absent frequently because of imaginary ailments. This may become a pattern. They fall behind in their classes, miss more and more education every year, grow progressively unhappier with school and finally drop out. Studies have shown that dropouts often exhibit a pattern of absenteeism as early as the first or second grade. Try to remedy any problems early in your child's school years, and be sure that absences and skipping school don't undermine his education.

Be careful about your attitude toward school when you talk to your child. Don't mention how much you disliked school and how you played hooky with the gang. Don't let your child skip school to go shopping or stay home as a treat. Instead, keep a positive attitude, expecting that he will both like and do well in school. It is part of your responsibility as a parent to see that your child goes to school every day unless he is too ill to attend.

Keep an eye on the work your child brings home to see how he's doing. It's wise to set up a file for each child, to date work as it is brought home and to keep this work throughout the school year. As you add new tests, worksheets, and artwork to the file, glance at the previous work. Is there a pattern to grades or teacher comments? Is the work improving? Getting worse? If scores are slowly getting better, be sure to compliment your child. If the work seems to be deteriorating or shows no improvement, talk to your child and determine if you need to speak with the teacher. As your child brings work home, try to find something about it to discuss and to praise. Surprisingly, most parents give their children little praise in spite of the fact that praise builds self-esteem and is a greater motivator than criticism and nagging.

Lessening the Trauma of Report Card Time

If you ask adults to remember the most stressful times in their childhood, report card time will probably rank near the top. Report cards are often a major cause of strife between parents and children, but they shouldn't be. Parents should have a general idea of how their children are doing before they get report cards. They should remember that report cards are a measure of how students are doing in school, not of students' worth as individuals or of parents' success as parents. Also, report cards measure what has happened in the past; they show what is over and can't be changed. For this reason, if report cards are not good, they should be used as a platform for change rather than as a reason for punishment. If you ground your child because of a bad report card—or if you yell and scream and tell him he is lazy or stupid—you will be doing nothing to improve his grades, and in fact you will probably make the situation worse. Much more effective is a calm discussion of the grades and the working out of plans with your child, and with his teacher, if necessary, to improve them.

If you've been careful to check the work your child brings home, and to listen and talk to him about his progress, you should have a good idea of what to expect on his report cards. If your child's tests and homework show B minuses and C pluses, then you shouldn't be surprised that report cards show B minuses and C pluses, too. Or, if your usually straight-A child begins to bring home tests with D's and C's on them, be prepared for a report card that is not up to its usual standards.

Of course not all report cards will be bad. A good one should be a time for praise and congratulations. Experts caution against rewarding children for good grades—ten dollars for an A, for example—because they think this harms self-motivation. Though these experts say that praise is better than cash, many parents do reward children for good grades. Even if your child's report card isn't as good as you would like, look for something positive—a grade raised in math, or a teacher's comment about how hard he is working—and show your child that you are pleased with whatever successful efforts he *is* demonstrating. Too many parents overlook the strengths in their child's report card, focusing only on the problem areas.

Besides finding something to praise in your child's report

card, look for trends. At least once or twice a year, get out all the cards from the current and previous years and compare them. Do you see a pattern—possibly slow but steady signs of improvement, or a sudden drop in grades? Usually a single grade is less important than where it fits in relation to previous grades, so be sure to keep all report cards.

Most schools issue report cards two to four times a year, and most still use letter grades, ranging from the traditional A (excellent) to F (failing). Some schools add a plus or a minus to letter grades, so there are greater possible variations. Some schools use a system of "satisfactory" or "unsatisfactory," or of "above average/average/below average." Some even use a check mark with a plus (√+) for above average and a check mark with a minus (√−) for below average. A few schools don't use grades at all, particularly in the early elementary years. Instead, parents receive written comments from the teacher. Some high schools also allow pass/fail grades for elective classes.

Grades should give you an overall idea of how well students are doing in their subjects. They shouldn't reflect students' behavior unless that behavior affects their grades. In other words, teachers shouldn't try to punish students through their grades. Thus, students should not be graded down in English because they talk out of turn in class. Students also shouldn't receive higher grades than they deserve because they are obedient or "nice." Most elementary school report cards have a section in which teachers can comment on classroom behavior, citizenship and peer relations. If your child is graded down for a reason unrelated to academic progress, such as for misbehavior, you should discuss the grade with his teacher and try to work out a better way of controlling the unacceptable behavior.

You may wonder what place effort has in grading. Teachers will tell you that they know which students are working to the best of their ability and which are just slipping by.

They will probably also tell you that they expect more from a highly talented student than from an average one. Thus, very bright students who are working below their potential can expect to receive lower grades than those working their hardest. Still, effort should not have a heavy influence on grades, since grades should reflect performance; rather, effort is often the factor that determines whether a borderline grade will go up or down.

Generally, individual teachers decide how to weight grades. For example, one teacher may decide that 50 percent of the grade will hinge on tests, 25 percent on homework and 25 percent on class participation, while another will decide that 60 percent hinges on tests, 25 percent on homework and 15 percent on class participation. Your child should know the weighting system used in each of his classes, and you will want to learn them if you're concerned about specific grades. If you are uncertain, ask at the start of the year or during parent-teacher conferences how teachers weight grades.

What should you do if you are worried about your child's progress based on his report cards, or if you believe one or more grades are incorrect? Start by discussing the situation with him. If it's a matter of generally low grades, try to find out what the problem is. Review tests and papers your child has brought home—this is one of many times when a file for each child will come in handy. Are the grades on the papers and tests in keeping with the grades on the report card? Does there seem to be a problem with one aspect of your child's performance (with tests, for example), or do comments and grades on homework show that there is a special problem here? Then think about your child's study habits. Is his homework done every night? Does he claim there was none assigned or always say that he has done it all? Does he do his homework in front of the TV? Are spelling words learned at the last minute, or well in advance of a weekly test? At breakfast, does your child suddenly remember assignments that should have been completed the night before? If any of these are problems, work with him on solving them. This may require helping him to set up a study schedule and deciding that all homework must be finished before the TV set is turned on.

If you don't know what the problem is or how to solve it, or if you question a specific grade, you'll want to talk to the teacher. In this case, phone the school office and leave a message for the teacher to return your call. Don't expect a teacher to leave class to talk to you, but do expect that the teacher will get back to you within a reasonable time. If you don't hear from the teacher within a couple of days, call again, because messages can go astray.

You may be able to discuss a relatively simple problem with the teacher over the phone. For example, you may just need an explanation of what was meant by a written comment on a report card. More likely, though, you'll want to set up a parent-teacher conference to discuss the problem at greater length. Although occasionally students are involved in such conferences, most likely it will just be the teacher and one or, better yet, both parents. If your child has several teachers, you may need to set up separate conferences. This is time consuming but well worth the effort.

Making Parent-Teacher Conferences Work

For many mothers and fathers, parent-teacher conferences, whether requested to discuss a special problem or regularly scheduled by the school once or twice a year, are times of tension, fear and frustration. Parents are afraid that they will hear unpleasant things about their child. They are worried that they won't know what to say or will ask stupid questions. Some fear that the teacher will verbally attack them or their child. Others are frustrated because the time is so short that they can't get answers to all their questions.

Although a certain amount of apprehension is natural, it may make you feel better to know that teachers are also anxious about talking to parents. In a recent Metropolitan Life/Harris poll of American teachers, 55 percent said they were hesitant about contacting parents to discuss problems, while only 20 percent of parents were reluctant to contact teachers. Also realize that since many teachers are parents themselves, they have to go through what you do when they talk to their own child's teachers. Therefore, most teachers know how uncomfortable you probably feel.

Conferences are easier and more useful when parents and teachers already know each other. It's a good idea to make a point of meeting the teacher at the start of the school year. School- and PTA-sponsored open houses or social events like spaghetti suppers are other times for parents and teachers to get acquainted. Parents shouldn't hesitate to introduce themselves at such an event, but this is not the occasion to try to solve any problems.

Doing volunteer work in the classroom is an excellent way of getting to know a teacher and learning what happens in school. Parent volunteers get opportunities to discuss their child's problems and successes in the normal course of conversation. This helps parents learn about problems before report card time and get a general idea of their child's progress. Teachers welcome many kinds of assistance, from helping with paperwork and collecting lunch money to tutoring students and speaking to a class about careers or hobbies. Almost all PTAs organize parent volunteers for the school such as by designating room representatives, who help the classroom teacher with special projects and serve as the PTA link to parents in that class. If your schedule permits, contact the teacher or PTA room representative and offer your services.

When a conference is scheduled, talk to your child about it. Many youngsters are apprehensive upon learning that their parents are to meet with their teacher, so offer reassurance that the conference will center around helping, not comparing notes about what they may have done wrong at home or school. Ask your child about the subjects he likes best and least; any subjects that are giving him trouble; how he gets along with his classmates and teacher; and what, if any, problems need to be addressed. If report cards are a special concern, discuss this carefully with your child. For example, ask why he thinks math is giving him trouble. What could help him do better? What would he like his teacher to know?

You should take a few minutes prior to the meeting to think about your child—his strengths and weaknesses, and his study and learning habits. Consider whether he is shy, whether he approaches new learning situations with eagerness or fear, how well he adapts to new situations and how thoroughly he concentrates on homework. Also think about whether you are helping enough with his homework.

Once again review the file of the work brought home by your child. Bring along papers or tests about which you have questions or that show a particular problem. If your school has a parent/student handbook, read it carefully. Flip through your child's textbooks. Think about what your child has told you about his teacher. Is there something of a positive nature that you could relate, that your child has said about the teacher or the class? While your aim is not to butter up the teacher, beginning with a compliment or a simple thank you for the teacher's hard work will reduce tension and create the kind of pleasant atmosphere that makes genuine communication possible.

Jot down questions you want answered at the conference. Even if you are concerned about just one area, take advantage of the opportunity to discuss your child's all-around performance, too. While questions will differ depending on the child and his age, here are some the National PTA suggests you consider:

- What are my child's best and worst subjects? What can I do to help him improve in weak areas or to do even better in his best areas?
- Is my child working up to his ability? If not, why not, and what can you suggest to help?
- Is my child making good progress in his subjects? If he is falling behind, what can be done to help him catch up? If he is well ahead of other students, what can be done to encourage and challenge him more?
- How does my child get along with his classmates? Are there any problems? Does he participate in group activities? Is he unusually shy? Too aggressive? Does he seem to have friends among the other children?
- How does my child get along with you and other teachers? Are there any special behavior or learning problems that I should be aware of? Does he participate in class discussions as well as talk about interests and activities?
- Have you noticed any recent changes in either my child's behavior or schoolwork? Do you see any signs (tiredness, moodiness, vision trouble) of possible emotional or physical problems?
- What kinds of tests are being given this year? When are they scheduled? What are the tests supposed to tell and what have they said about my child thus far?
- Is my child's homework turned in on time, in completed form and well done? Is there any continuing homework problem that I can help remedy?
- How much time each night should my child spend on homework?
- Has my child had any unexplained absences, or is there an attendance problem?

If you have questions concerning school policies or school programs that might help your child, this is the time to ask them. You should pass along information about your child that you would like the teacher to have, mentioning any illnesses, divorce, recent moves or other family situations or problems that might be stressful for your child.

Both parents should attend the conference if at all possible. Be on time and prepared to ask your most important questions first, in case time runs out. If only one of you can be there, it is up to that parent to pass along the questions and comments of the other. Many schools now schedule conferences at times convenient for working parents. If that is not the case in your school, try to arrange the meeting when everyone is available, or see if your employer will allow time off from work. Parent-teacher conferences are so important that they should never be missed, even if you have to take vacation time to attend.

You may want to see samples of your child's work, especially if he is having trouble. If you are ever unclear about what any teacher is telling you, continue to ask questions or request explanations until you understand. Most importantly, though, be sure to stay calm. Arguing and blaming each other for his problems will do nothing to develop a good parent-teacher relationship or to help your child learn.

Probably the most important part of a good parent-teacher conference occurs when you and the teacher decide about what, if anything, needs to be done to help your child. Possibilities include homework aids, special attention to his interests and strengths, tutoring, assistance by a counselor or other school staff member, extra parent help with homework or follow-up meetings between you and the teacher. The conference should not be concluded until you both have reached an agreement on what needs to be done and how to begin.

After the conference, discuss with your child what was talked about and any arrangements that were made. He should understand what you and his teacher are trying to accomplish, and why. It's best to begin immediately to implement the

TEN STEPS TO A GOOD PARENT-TEACHER CONFERENCE

1. Get to know your child's teacher early in the school year, before conferences are scheduled or problems develop.
2. Plan for conferences. Talk to your child. Jot down questions. Glance over your child's textbooks and work he brings home. Think about your child's learning style and study habits.
3. Have both parents attend the conference if possible.
4. Ask questions about your child's schoolwork; his relationship with students and teachers; tests taken or scheduled; and any class or school rules you don't understand.
5. Stay calm. Don't get angry or defensive, argue, or try to assess blame. Concentrate instead on developing a good working relationship with the teacher.
6. Share with the teacher any information that might develop an understanding of your children.
7. Decide with the teacher what, if anything, needs to be done to help your child. Agree on plans and on any special assistance that your child needs before you leave.
8. Talk with your child afterward and discuss what was decided.
9. Follow up. Implement your end of any agreement. Keep in touch with the teacher. If the plan doesn't seem to be working, or if new problems develop, call the teacher and ask for another meeting.
10. Ask for other help if you aren't getting results. If the teacher isn't helpful or progress isn't being made, talk with a supervisor. Call the principal's office to see whom you should talk to next.

plans. Stay in touch with the teacher to assess your child's progress.

If problems remain unresolved, or if new ones develop at any time, contact the school again. If you are still unsatisfied after an additional conference with a teacher, or if you fail to see results, make an appointment with the teacher's supervisor. A call to the principal's office, with a brief explanation of the problem, will identify the next step for you to take. This may mean meeting with the principal, with an assistant principal or with a department head. In most cases, though, you will find that you and the teacher will be able to work out problems together.

Setting the Record Straight

Once a year when you go to the school for a parent-teacher conference, it's a good idea to check your child's records (sometimes called cumulative records). You should call the school office a week or two before your conference and ask the secretary to have the records available for you either before or after the conference. Otherwise, office staff may be too busy to accommodate you on the spur of the moment.

The passage by Congress in 1974 of the Buckley Amendment, which the National PTA supported, means that if your child attends a school receiving federal funds, you have the right to see all his school records. Until this amendment was passed, schools often withheld this information from parents, even though they sometimes let other groups such as the FBI or even potential employers see these records. Now all records are open to parents, and there can be no confidential files for use by school personnel only. You may challenge material in the records if you believe it is inaccurate or irrelevant. If the school does not change or delete disputed material, you can ask to add explanatory material, or you can request an impartial hearing before a school official who is not directly involved in the dispute.

Records may not be released to anyone outside the school without parental approval except in an emergency or except for the kind of information that would be printed in a school directory—name, address, date of birth, school activities, etc. This law does not give you the right to see the personal notes of teachers, counselors or administrators as long as they do not make them a part of your child's records or share them generally with others in the school. In the case of a divorce, the law gives both the parent with custody and the parent without custody the right to see the records, unless the school receives a court order denying access to such information to one parent.

Why should you be concerned? When you look at your child's records, you will most likely find everything in order. There will be information about tests and grades plus records of immunizations and medical exams. If your child has been referred to a counselor or enrolled in a special education program, you'll find a more extensive file. Check the accuracy of all these records. You may find, for example, that your child has gone through seven years of schooling with the wrong spelling of his first name. Ask the school secretary to make minor corrections for you.

What you should *not* find in your child's records are comments such as "Parents are involved in a messy divorce" or "Child is incorrigible" or "Parents are pushy and like to make trouble." If you find such a notation, you'll need to learn how to challenge and change the records. The school must provide you with information about your rights and what procedures to take. Ask for a copy of those procedures if you do not have one. The school must also inform parents of their right to see all their child's records each year. Again, don't expect a problem, but plan on checking these records once a year to see that everything is in order.

Scott's in the 84th Percentile

The "excellence in education," or reform movement of the 1980s, has put new emphasis on testing to evaluate how well students and schools are doing. Also over the last decade, more than thirty states have instituted *minimum competency exams*—exams that students must pass before they can graduate from high school or before they can be promoted from one grade to another. For these reasons, your child will probably be taking more tests, and these tests will be increasingly important not only in measuring school progress but also in shaping important educational decisions.

Although parents recognize the importance of tests, they are probably more confused about testing than about any other part of their child's education. You may want to ask your local PTA president to schedule a meeting on testing early in the school year and to ask school staff to discuss the testing program with parents. (See the glossary of testing terms on pages 88–89 and the suggested additional readings at the end of this book.)

Parents are usually most uncertain about the meaning of *standardized achievement tests* used to measure what students have learned or what skills they can use in certain subjects. These tests are taken by millions of children across the nation. In order to standardize the conditions under which students take the tests, children are given the same amount of time in which to take the test, and teachers are provided with the same directions to explain the test. These tests are usually sent to the test maker to be graded. Because these tests are "standardized," and because they are given to many children, they allow students to be compared with others both in their school and across the nation.

Many parents have trouble understanding the scores their child makes on such tests. For example, you might receive a note from the school telling you that your fourth grader, Scott, has taken the Stanford Achievement Test and is in the 62nd *percentile* and 6th *stanine* overall—with a math score of 84th percentile and 7th stanine, and a reading score of 45th percentile and 5th stanine. Then you're told to call the school office if you have any questions. In some cases you might be told other information, such as your child's *raw score* (the number of questions answered correctly) and his *grade equivalency*. The note might also say that the test was *norm-referenced* rather than *criterion-referenced*. It might tell you a little about the *reliability* of the test (how well its results agree with results from other tests that are so similar that they should have the same results) and its *validity* (whether it actually tests what it should be testing). If you are like most parents, you won't even know where to begin to ask questions. You might consider just putting the test results into your file and forgetting them. Don't! These scores can be understood if you look at them piece by piece. And if you study them, you will find that they have a lot of valuable information about how your child is doing in school.

Let's look at this hypothetical test result in more detail. The name of the test is the Stanford Achievement Test. There are many different standardized tests, some named after the university or state where they were developed, or after the company that makes them. In addition to the Stanford test, the Iowa and California are others that are used often. Unless you have some specific reason for concern, you can generally leave questions about the type of test, its reliability and its validity to the school staff in charge of selecting tests, concentrating instead on your child's performance.

The term "percentile" does not indicate the percentage of right answers. It means the percent of children that your child scored equal to or above. Your child will usually receive an overall score as well as specific scores for subjects tested (in this example, reading and math). So an overall score of 62nd percentile means that your child did as well as or better than 62 percent of the group of children with whom he is being compared. Looking at this another way, only 38 percent of students did better than your child; therefore, your child scored well above average. The percentile of 84 in math means that your child did as well as or better than 84 percent of the children in the comparison group, and only 16 percent did better. The reading score of 45th percentile shows that your child did slightly worse than average, with 55 percent of all children doing better.

If your child fit this example, you might be concerned about the large gap in performance between the 84th percentile in math and the 45th percentile in reading. You might want to talk with the teacher about ways to help him with reading. Also, you'll want to check what groups your child is being compared with. If only one set of percentiles is given, this generally means that your child is being compared with a nationwide sample or group of children (usually called the norm group) who took the test at some time in the past.

You don't need to worry about the stanine scores if you understand the percentiles, since stanines give less specific information than do percentiles. If only stanines are given, ask the teacher or the school staff member in charge of testing to translate them into percentiles. Generally speaking, stanines of 1 to 3 are below average, 4 to 6 are average, and 7 to 9 are above average.

The grade equivalency is one of the most difficult parts of the testing puzzle. If the fourth grader in our example took the test in October, his actual grade would be listed as 4.2, that is, the fourth year, second month. If he scored the grade equivalent (GE) of 4.9, his score would be equal to that of an average fourth grader in the norm group who was currently in the ninth month (May) of the school year. This would not necessarily indicate, though, that he could do the work expected of a student at this level, since he might not have learned all the skills that would have been taught in the intervening seven months.

If your child scores a year or two higher than his actual grade, don't assume that he should be pushed ahead a year or two. No decision to advance a child should be based on test scores alone. If your child's grade equivalency is two or three years below where he actually is, you probably need to talk to the teacher. There may be a problem with the test. For example, your school may not have taught all the material covered in the test. Your child may have just had a bad day, and the test may not have shown what he really knows. Or, the test may have pinpointed a genuine problem. Before talking to the teacher, though, you should be aware that grade equivalency scores are so often misunderstood or misleading that many test makers are suggesting that they no longer be used. So take grade equivalency scores with a particularly large grain of salt.

Most of the standardized tests your child takes will probably be norm-referenced tests rather than criterion-referenced tests. In a norm-referenced test a sample or selection of students is drawn from the nation or state or even school district. Then your child's score is compared with that group, or "norm." So standardized achievement tests that compare one student to other students are called norm referenced. The other type of test—criterion referenced—doesn't compare students. Instead, it measures what individual students know about a subject, for example, how well an individual student can multiply or do fractions. If you are told that your child met seventeen out of twenty-three objectives in reading, he took a criterion-referenced test. Scores on criterion-referenced tests will not tell you anything about how your child compared with other children.

There are many other types of tests, including *IQ tests*, *aptitude tests*, *interest tests*, and *personality (attitude) tests*. The best known of all these kinds of tests is the *SAT*, *Scholastic Aptitude Test,* which students take during their junior or senior year of high school. Most students take either the SAT (the College Board's Scholastic Aptitude Test) or the ACT (the American College Testing Program). These tests attempt to predict how well students will do in the freshman year of college. Many colleges and universities use them along with class rank and teacher recommendations to help decide which students to accept. Colleges rely on them because grades differ so widely from one school to another. Since colleges can't know that a B in one high school where teachers are tough graders is worth more than an A from another school where standards are not as high, scholastic aptitude tests are

TESTING TERMS

Achievement tests—tests that measure how much students have learned about a subject or what skills they have mastered.

ACT—American College Testing Program, used by many colleges to help determine admission eligibility.

Aptitude tests—tests that measure abilities or skills that aren't closely linked to a particular subject or course.

Classroom tests—quizzes or exams usually made up and graded by the classroom teacher that are used to motivate students to study, evaluate their work and learn students' strengths and weaknesses.

Criterion-referenced tests—tests that measure how well students do in a subject, or what skills they have mastered. Such tests do not compare students with other students.

Grade equivalency—scores consisting of two numbers separated by a decimal point. The first represents the grade in school, and the second indicates the school month. This system allows scores of students to be translated to the performance level typical of students in the recorded grade at the given time of the year. Thus, if a student had a grade equivalency of 5.5, this would mean that he scored as well as the average student in the comparison group in the fifth month of the fifth grade.

Interest tests—tests of students' interests or what they like best. Such tests are often used to help students decide what career to pursue.

IQ tests—tests that aim to determine students' "intelligence quotient," or mental ability.

❦ ❦ ❦

supposed to give them a more accurate way of evaluating students. The guidance counselor at your child's school can give you more information about the SAT, ACT and other aptitude exams.

Minimum competency exams—exams that must be passed for students to graduate or be promoted into certain grades. Such tests are now required by more than thirty states.

Norm-referenced tests—tests that allow comparison between those students currently taking them and a sample group of students (the norm) who have taken them at some time in the past.

Percentile—a measure of the percentage of students in the norm group that a student's score is equal to or above.

Personality tests—tests designed to reveal students' personality, attitudes, motivations or other characteristics.

Raw score—the number of questions answered correctly on an exam.

Readiness tests—tests of physical, mental, and language development and maturity that are administered to assess students' readiness for kindergarten or first grade. Some states now require such tests.

Reliability—a measure of how well test results agree with the results of other tests whose design is so similar that they should have the same results.

SAT—Scholastic Aptitude Test, which measures skills useful for predicting how well students will do in their freshman year in college. This test helps determine college admissions.

Standardized tests—tests that are given under "controlled" or similar circumstances so that all students have an equal chance. They allow students to be compared with other students.

Stanine—a single-digit number that is sometimes used to report scores. A 9 is the highest, a 1 is the lowest, and a 5 is average.

Validity—a measure of whether a test actually gauges what it should.

What Tests Can and Cannot Tell You

Many educators charge that tests are not good evaluators of what students really know or what they can do. Some critics claim that tests, especially scholastic aptitude and IQ tests, are biased against minorities and disadvantaged students as well as against women. Others say that today's emphasis on testing means that too much school time is taken away from what schools are supposed to be doing—educating students. So tests are surrounded by controversy.

But tests can be useful tools to assess how well students are doing in school, to assure that teaching is on target and to diagnose students' problems. Keep in mind, though, that tests measure students' performance on a certain sample of questions at a particular time. Although every effort is made to standardize tests, the scores might be different if your child took them on a different day or if different people administered them in different circumstances. Thus, tests must be interpreted cautiously. "Educational tests are useful but not perfect," says Gregory Anrig, president of the Educational Testing Service (ETS) and a member of the National PTA's board of directors. "Test results are most useful when considered in combination with other information about students. Parents and teachers should understand tests and their limitations if they are to be used properly to benefit students."

To make the best use of test scores, look for general trends or a score that is markedly out of line with others. If your child's overall percentile on achievement tests has dropped from 63 to 47 in four years, talk to school personnel to see if this drop indicates a problem. Likewise, if your child's score is markedly lower in one subject than in others, see if he needs extra help in the weak area. If, on the other hand, scores on several tests show that your child does particularly well in one area, he may have a special talent that can be further developed. Finally, if test results are way out of line with what you think your child's abilities are, discuss this with his teacher or with other school staff. Don't attach too much importance to any one score.

Scores can give you an idea of what you can realistically expect from your child. All parents want their children to be superstars, but some are not. While you want to help yours do his best, you must accept his limitations as well as his strengths. Some parents see test scores that they don't like and immediately say the scores are wrong. In some cases this is true, but in others the parents are wrong, not the scores. So consider what scores mean and find out what, if anything, teachers and the school plan to do with them. Do they think changes need to be made in the way the material is taught or in what is covered? Do they think your child needs special assistance or special programs? Most likely the scores will merely confirm teachers' observations. If the school or teachers believe that the test scores require significant changes in your child's schooling, though, you will want to be informed and to participate in planning for such changes. And remember, some children just don't test well. If your child doesn't, test scores will be less useful.

Help Your Child Do His Best

Because children's test scores can vary significantly, you will want to do everything you can to help your child do his best on tests. Find out early in the school year what kind of major tests will be given and when. Mark the dates on your calendar. Be sure your child has a quiet, restful weekend and a good night's sleep before he takes the test. Get him up early enough on test mornings so he doesn't have to rush, and encourage him to eat a good breakfast. Before he goes off to school, wish him luck and tell him that you know he will do well.

If your child is very young, talk to him a little about the test. Especially if this is his first standardized test, you'll want to let him know that tests are important and that he should do his best, but don't put heavy pressure on him. Instead, let him know that although tests need to be treated seriously, he should not be afraid of them.

For both young and older children, the most important thing they can do on a test is to listen to what the teacher tells them. Remind your child to read or listen to the directions carefully and to ask the teacher to repeat any instructions that are unclear. If the directions permit, suggest that he glance briefly through a test before starting to get an idea of its length. Advise him to watch the time carefully, not spending too long on any one problem. If stuck, he should mark the problem so he can return to it, but meanwhile keep moving through the material. Tell him to use all the time allowed. If he finishes early, he should go back to check his work, especially those areas that seem the hardest.

If your child is ready for college entrance exams or scholastic aptitude tests, you might suggest some special preparation, since study or coaching can improve a student's score. He can check to see if the guidance counselor has a book or computer software with sample questions, or he can borrow a book from the library or buy one at a bookstore. If students take some sample timed tests, they can become familiar with the kinds of questions they are likely to face as well as get a sense of how fast they will have to move through the test. This will relieve some of their anxiety and get them used to the test format. Also, remember that students can take SAT exams a second time if they feel their score was too low; some colleges will consider only the higher score, while others will average the two.

In the long run you can best help your child prepare for tests by seeing that he develops good study and work habits, keeps up with class and homework assignments, and reads as much as possible. In particular, when children pay careful attention to directions, keep track of time and use it wisely, avoid careless errors and review their work whenever they study, these same skills and practices will stand them in good stead at test time.

You can also encourage your child to develop a positive attitude toward tests. Help him understand that tests are just one aspect of schooling. Be careful not to overemphasize test results. If he doesn't feel that you are judging his worth on the basis of test scores, or that his whole future rides on how well he does, he will be less fearful about tests and probably perform better.

Part of your child's attitude toward tests depends on how you discuss the results with him. Again, don't make a big deal of test scores or reproach your child for his performance. Discuss instead how the test shows strengths as well as areas that might be improved. Look at how his test scores have changed through the years and find something to praise. Remind your child and yourself that tests are administered to gather information to help children learn, and that they paint only one part of the picture of how well your child is doing in school.

What—My *Child Flunking?*

If your child is not doing well in school, especially in kindergarten or the early elementary grades, the teacher may discuss the possibility of retaining rather than promoting him. More often the child to be retained is a boy, since boys mature more slowly than girls at this stage. When the issue of possible retention is first raised, your reaction will probably be horror. Once the shock subsides, you should ask yourself, "What is best for my child—repeating the grade or being promoted?"

For many years, educators have been sharply divided on whether retention works, but recent research against retention is piling up. John Stammer, a University of Toledo professor who has studied retention, wrote on the subject for *PTA Today* magazine. He cited research studies showing that either retaining or promoting a child will help him only about half the time. In other words, there is no overwhelming evidence that holding a child back a year will let him catch up. Likewise, there's no overwhelming evidence that he will catch up on his own even if promoted. One thing the research does show is that retention has very little benefit for older children. If it works at all, it works only for kindergarten, first or second grades. In fact, one study found that children who are retained after the first grade never seem to catch up. But in spite of the findings, many school districts still have retention policies.

If there is a possibility that your child will be retained, the teacher should inform you of that as early in the year as possible, by midyear at the latest. If you're concerned about your child's progress, keep in close contact with the teacher from the very start of the school year. When the teacher first mentions possible retention, ask why your child is having problems. Is he having trouble learning? Is he socially immature and unable to work with other children? Is he not adjusting to the school routine? Most often the answer will be that the child is not learning as quickly as he should.

Once the teacher explains this, ask how you and the teacher can work together to help him catch up, enabling him to continue with his class. Will tutoring help? Is there a summer program that could serve as a bridge to the next grade?

Next ask the teacher what kind of program the child would have if he were retained. Studies have shown that it doesn't help children to be recycled through the same class, the same teacher and the same material. Would your child have a different teacher and program the second year? Ask whether there are remedial programs he could take advantage of if he were promoted. Would these programs help him catch up to the level of his class? Is there any kind of a transition class, or is there a possibility of partial promotion so that the child could be promoted but helped to cover some of the material from the previous grade? Will the school prepare a written plan for the child if he is retained, enabling a new teacher to help him learn most effectively, or will it provide a plan for helping him with remedial services if he is promoted?

The attitudes of family members and friends will be very important whether the child is ultimately retained or promoted. Although educators now use the term "retained" or "held back" rather than "flunked," a strong stigma is still attached. Children older than kindergartners long remember who wasn't promoted. For children who are retained, this may be the first major failure in life, setting a pattern that continues throughout their school career. Parents can lessen the feeling of failure if they calmly discuss retention with their child, if they are supportive and if they help their child find other ways to succeed.

Sometimes the school will be uncertain about whether to retain or promote a child and will ask parents for their opinion. David Elkind, former president of the National Association for the Education of Young Children, writes in *Miseducation,* "Given the new data on negative effects of retention showing that socially promoted children [children promoted just to keep them with others of their age group] do as well as children who are held back, you might want to insist that your son be promoted." If you do recommend or insist upon promotion, be sure that the child gets extra help to catch up. If you and the school agree that the child should be retained, insist that it prepare a program, preferably in writing, to help your child make the most of this extra year.

PTAs in Action

Most PTAs encourage parents to serve as classroom tutors and aides, library aides, trip chaperons, playground monitors, guest speakers, picture persons (parent volunteers who provide information about art, including famous paintings), etc. Many PTAs conduct programs to improve parent-teacher relations and to help parents learn how their children are doing in school. Here are some examples:

• The Spring Garden Elementary PTA in Bedford, Texas, established a volunteer program that included a fall recruitment. Volunteers work in the library, classrooms and computer lab. The PTA orients and trains volunteers, coordinates their work, evaluates volunteer programs and recognizes outstanding volunteers.

• The White Oak PTA in White Oak, Pennsylvania, held a program entitled "Why We Test and How to Interpret Results."

• The Howard County PTA Council in Maryland asked its school district to revise report cards in elementary schools, and it offered suggestions for improvement. The district agreed to issue new report cards that make it easier for parents to tell how well their children are doing.

• The Oyster School in Washington, D.C., is a bilingual elementary school with a very diverse student body. To help parents and teachers work more closely together, its PTA invited all parents and teachers to attend a Saturday workshop entitled "Building the Partnership." Facilitators were selected to help groups discuss topics such as testing, discipline and homework from both the parents' and the teachers' perspective.

• The Shawnee Mission East PTA in Shawnee Mission, Kansas, helps schedule parent-teacher conferences and provides baby-sitting on conference days and nights.

• The Milwaukee City PTA Council has published a brochure entitled *Talking to Your Child's Teacher* in both English and Spanish.

CHAPTER

5

Helping Your Child Learn

IF YOU'RE LIKE most parents, you are probably looking for the key to helping your child do well in school. So you ask yourself, "Will a home computer or a set of encyclopedias or a speed-reading course help Jessica keep her grade point up now that she is going into junior high? Will summer school or a tutor help Ryan with math?"

There is no single key to academic success for your child, but there are several important ways that you can help her do her best in school. You can establish a home atmosphere that encourages a child to learn and to like and to do well in school. You can show your child that education and learning are important to you and to her future. You can take an active role in her education by reading to her and helping her with her homework. And, you can help her develop self-esteem.

Self-Esteem Is Key

Self-esteem, which plays a tremendously important role in your child's life, is something she must develop long before setting foot in school. From parents and other family members as well as from child-care providers and friends, children

TEN THINGS TEACHERS WISH PARENTS WOULD DO

1. **Be involved in their children's education.** Parents' involvement helps students learn, improves schools and makes teachers' jobs easier.
2. **Provide resources at home for reading and learning.** Parents should have books and magazines for their children and read to or with their children each day.
3. **Set a good example.** Parents should show their children that they believe reading is both enjoyable and useful. They shouldn't spend all their time in front of the TV, either.
4. **Encourage children to do their best in school.** Parents must indicate that they believe education is important and that they want their children to do the best they possibly can at school.
5. **Emphasize academics.** Too many parents get caught up in athletics and in preparing their children for the world of work, when academics should be their first concern.
6. **Support school rules and goals.** Parents should take care not to undermine school rules, discipline or goals.
7. **Use pressure positively.** Parents should encourage children to do their best, but they should not apply too much pressure, by setting unattainable goals or by involving them in too many activities.
8. **Call teachers early if there is a problem** (not wait for teachers to call them), so there is still time to improve the situation.
9. **Accept their responsibility as parents,** and not expect the school and teachers to take over this job. For example, parents should make it their responsibility to teach children basic discipline at home rather than to leave this task to teachers.
10. **View drinking by underage youth and excessive partying as a serious matter, not a joke.** Drinking, partying and staying out late take a toll on students' classroom performance. While parents are concerned about drug abuse, many fail to recognize that alcohol is the drug most frequently abused by youngsters as well as adults.

fashion their personal assessment of their own worth, that is, their self-esteem. Children who feel that they are loved, respected and taken seriously, and who feel that they are responsible for and able to influence their lives, generally have high self-esteem. Such children usually make the most of their abilities.

Success in school is so heavily linked to self-esteem that a student with a high IQ but low self-esteem may do poorly, while a child with average intelligence but high self-esteem may excel. High self-esteem doesn't just pay off in school. Critical decisions such as whether to use drugs, to drop out of school or to become sexually active are affected by children's sense of self-worth, as are many of their other personal and career decisions. Also, children with low self-esteem are usually afraid to try new things or to accept challenges, which means that they often become underachievers. So helping your child develop high self-esteem is one of the most important things you can do for her.

There are many ways to foster self-esteem in your child. While your efforts will be most effective if you start when she is an infant, it is never too late to build her self-esteem and to improve your communication with her. Showing your child how to communicate her feelings openly and honestly is a good place to begin. Children need to know that even anger and fear are normal, and that these feelings shouldn't be bottled up inside them. Since children learn by example, parents must let their own feelings be known in positive ways.

Truly listening to a child is important for developing her self-esteem. When you listen to her, she feels good about herself, and she also learns how to listen to siblings, her teacher, other children and you. Hearing what other people have to say helps a child to cooperate, to negotiate and to compromise—all of which are important in developing self-esteem. Help your child learn these difficult skills by showing her how to work out her problems peacefully and by praising her when she cooperates with her siblings or other children. Show her how to anticipate others' feelings and responses by learning to put herself into their shoes.

Fair, consistent discipline is another building block of self-esteem. The purpose of discipline should be to teach children to make wise decisions rather than to punish them for misconduct. For this reason, you should establish necessary rules but not make too many of them. Too many rules, especially those imposed on youngsters without their participation in the rule formulation, make them feel powerless and hemmed in, resulting in low self-esteem.

Give your child responsibility—meaningful, "do-able" jobs for which they are accountable—and praise her when she completes her tasks. Never take your child's help for granted. If you give your child increasing amounts of responsibility and praise her for her successes, she will think of herself as a contributing member of the family, which will boost her self-esteem.

Although you probably wish that you could pour your years of experience into your child, you need to let her make her own decisions—including occasional bad decisions. Only by paying the consequences for poor decisions will she learn to make good ones. Children who can make decisions feel good about themselves and believe that they have some control over their lives. This translates into high self esteem.

Praise is also important in developing your child's feelings of self-worth. Try to ignore unwanted behavior unless it is harming her or others, but don't ignore good behavior. Seek out opportunities to praise your child. Be especially careful not to call her lazy, bad, stupid, clumsy, or worthless, or to use other derogatory words. What you say in anger is often long remembered, and statements that you really don't mean may shape what your child thinks about herself.

Treat your child with love, humor, respect and courtesy. Treating her as a worthwhile individual will go a long way toward convincing her that she is in fact worthwhile. Treat your child as you yourself want to be treated. Building her self-esteem in this way will pay off at home, school and throughout her life.

Helping with Homework

Many recent studies have emphasized the role of homework in helping students learn and have noted that Japanese students spend about twice as much time doing homework as do their American counterparts. According to a U.S. Department of Education report entitled *What Works,* "Student achievement rises significantly when teachers regularly assign homework and students conscientiously do it." But studies have also found that homework is useful only when it is reviewed and returned promptly, and when it supplements what the students are learning in class. Homework should not be boring, repetitive drudgery. Good homework assignments cause students to practice newly learned skills, make them think about some aspect of their studies and increase their interest in school and the courses they are studying.

Homework is important because it helps students learn better, teaches them to make decisions and exercise their judgment, improves grades, makes them better readers, reinforces topics covered in class, and encourages them to be self-disciplined and responsible. Homework enables you to stay in touch with what your child is studying and gives you an excellent opportunity to be involved in her education. It is also the least expensive way to extend the length of the school day. *What Works* reports that students of average ability who do three to five hours of homework a week (notice, a week —not a night) usually get as good grades as students of high ability who do no homework; and students of low ability who do only one to three hours of homework a week usually get as high grades as students of average ability who do no homework.

While recognizing the importance of homework, many parents have questions about how much their child should be assigned and what they should do to help. The amount of time spent on homework should vary according to your child's age, abilities, work patterns, classes and teachers' requirements. Generally, students from kindergarten through the third grade have little homework. They may be asked to spend twenty minutes or so a night reading, printing lowercase letters, or adding and subtracting. More time than this is probably excessive.

Students in the fourth through the sixth grades should

FIFTEEN WAYS TO HELP YOUR CHILD LIKE HERSELF

1. Call attention to the good things your child does, not just the bad. Reward her for a job well done with praise, recognition, a special privilege or increased responsibility.
2. Show her that she is important to you. Talk with her about her activities and interests. Go to her games, concerts, parents' days at school and award ceremonies.
3. Take her ideas, emotions and feelings seriously. Don't laugh her concerns away by saying, "You'll grow out of it" or "It's not as bad as you think."
4. Set limits and clear rules, and enforce them, but don't hamstring your child with too many rules.
5. Use language that builds self-esteem, such as "What an excellent idea!" or "Thanks for your help. I could never have made it without you." Avoid language that destroys self-esteem: "Why are you so stupid?" or "How many times do I have to tell you something before you get it through your thick head?" or "You are absolutely worthless! I don't know why you were ever born."
6. Give your child responsibility so that she feels useful and valued.
7. Have reasonable expectations that your child can meet, and help her set reachable goals. Then praise her for her successes.

❦ ❦ ❦

be expected to do twenty to forty minutes of homework a day, though many teachers and schools assign more. There are no hard-and-fast rules for the length of time that junior high and senior high students should spend on homework, but some educators have suggested that high school students spend two hours a night on schoolwork. This would mean a major increase in the amount of time the average older American student would have to spend on homework, since most high school seniors report allocating only four or five hours a week to this activity, and a significant number do no homework at all.

Help your child with homework by starting when she is young to establish a quiet time each evening or after school.

8. Encourage your child to make her own decisions, and teach her that she must take responsibility for her actions and decisions.
9. Spend time with your child. Share favorite activities and be available when she needs you.
10. Discuss problems without placing blame or commenting negatively on your child's character. Look for ways to solve problems and prevent future ones rather than just deciding who was wrong.
11. Be sure to show your child your values. Instead of saying, "Do this" or "Don't do that," explain how your values and beliefs shape your behavior, and how beliefs and values can shape her life, too.
12. Be a good role model by showing your child that you feel good about yourself.
13. Teach your child to respect those with different backgrounds, values and experiences. Encourage her to value diversity and to look for friends from various groups of people.
14. Help your child learn to deal with time and money. Teach her to budget and spend wisely both of these important commodities.
15. Show how much you care for your child. Hug her. Tell her again and again that she is terrific and that you love her.

This time should be used for reading (or being read to), playing games or doing her homework. The practice will prepare her for more formal homework when she is older. Set up a place for her to work. A desk or table in her room is fine, but the kitchen table will work as well if distractions can be minimized and all family members recognize the need for quiet when one of them is studying. Some children can even study while lying on the floor or on their bed, but starting your child out at a desk or table is a better idea. As she gets older and becomes accustomed to the homework routine, she can adopt study habits that work for her.

Discourage your child from trying to work with the television on. Although many youngsters claim that they can do this, the practice invariably leads them to learn more about their favorite shows than about their history or math assignments. You'll have to consider your child's ability to concentrate before deciding whether to allow her to study with the radio or stereo on. Some students find that soft music cuts down on distractions, while for others music itself is a distraction.

Try to schedule homework sessions for a time when a parent is home. If this isn't possible, be sure to ask about homework, and check to see that it is completed every night. Find out if your community has a homework hotline that children can call if they are having problems or when their parents aren't available.

According to Grace Foster, a PTA leader from Granada Hills, California, "Your children will need more help with their homework when they are young. You may want to sit with very young students throughout their entire study time, going over directions and watching them work." If your child seems confused, go over the directions until she understands what is expected of her. Sometimes you may have trouble understanding the assignments as well. In that case, keep reading the directions and ask to look at textbooks that relate to the assignments. Once the directions are clear to you and your child, have her work one or two examples with you, and then let her work independently. Be ready to offer help as needed. "Don't fall into the trap of helping children so much that you wind up doing their homework for them," advises Foster. "The only way children will learn is if they do their work themselves."

As your child grows older, you will become less involved in the actual preparation of her homework, especially once she enters high school. At this stage, you should ask about assignments, help her understand her homework, be available for assistance if needed, monitor her progress during study time and check that all her homework has been completed. "You may want to help your children make a homework calendar, noting the days when reports or papers are due as well as when tests are scheduled," Foster continues. "It is also useful for students to jot down daily homework assignments in a small notebook. And be sure to discuss homework expectations and policies with your children's teachers during conferences," she adds.

Ask to see homework after teachers have returned it. Do this routinely for young children and occasionally even for high schoolers. Go over returned homework, discussing problems that the teacher has marked or praising your child for her progress. Put all returned homework, along with exams and other papers, into a file or folder that you review with your child from time to time. If she insists that no homework has been assigned, or that she finished it in study hall, ask that she spend the regular time reading, reviewing or working on an upcoming assignment.

When parents and teachers work together, they can help children develop good study habits and get the most possible out of their school years. Therefore, if your child is having problems with homework and cannot understand or complete assignments, or if she is constantly bored because the homework seems too easy, or if she never has homework, contact her teacher. You may also want to talk to the teacher if you find that the homework is not being checked and returned. You might ask your PTA president or the principal to call a meeting about homework so that parents can discuss problems and how to solve them. At such a meeting, you and other parents should consider whether your school needs a homework policy or a change in an existing policy.

Although homework is important, don't make too much of an issue of it. Like report cards, homework can cause major family battles. Avoid such battles by setting up rules when your child first starts school and insisting that they be followed. Don't nag or continually criticize your child about her homework. Don't get angry or use homework as an ex-

HOMEWORK TIPS FOR PARENTS

- Agree with your child on homework rules, such as when it must be done, where it should be done and what will happen if homework is not completed. Many parents insist that homework be finished before TV can be watched.
- Set up a place for your child to do her homework, such as a desk in her room or the kitchen table. Be sure that there is good light and that distractions are limited. Have necessary supplies including paper, pencils and a dictionary available.
- Expect your child to do homework each night. Ask her about homework assignments and show her that you think doing homework is an important responsibility.
- Try to schedule homework time for when you are at home, so that you can supervise and help your child. If this is not possible, be sure to check on her homework each night. Ask her to make a note of any problems that will require your assistance.
- Be sure that your child understands all homework assignments. If she has trouble, work an example out with her.
- Don't do your child's homework for her. Instead, work with her and encourage her to complete work herself.
- If your child is in elementary school, check, sign and date her homework each night.

❦ ❦ ❦

cuse to complain about other aspects of your child's life—such as a boyfriend you don't like or the fact that she didn't complete her household chores last night. Instead, expect that homework will be done, set high but realistic goals for your child, let her know these goals and be sure she understands that homework, like everything else in her education, is important to you. Finally, remind her that in the last analysis she alone is responsible for completing all her work.

Nurturing a Love of Reading

In many families, children spend hours and hours each day in front of the television set, but little time reading. *What Works* reports that the average elementary school student

- Be sure all homework is finished in proper form and in your child's backpack or book bag before she goes to bed. Nothing starts the day off worse than a mad scramble to complete a forgotten assignment or a hunt through the house for mislaid homework. And failing to complete homework or to take the finished product to school guarantees dissatisfied teachers as well as unprepared students.
- Keep track of your child's homework assignments and ask to see work that teachers have returned. Pay close attention to teachers' comments and look for any recurring problems.
- Contact your child's teachers if you don't understand their assignments or if your child has special problems. Also contact her teachers if they never assign homework.
- Discuss teachers' homework expectations during parent-teacher conferences and ask how much time your child should spend on homework each night.
- See if your school has a homework policy. If there seems to be a problem with homework in your school—too little or too much—ask your PTA president to discuss homework at an upcoming meeting or to call a special meeting for parents to discuss the topic.
- Don't forget to praise your child for a job well done when she completes her homework and when you see improvement.

spends only 7 or 8 minutes a day in silent reading at school, and even less at home. In fact, half of all fifth-grade students spend only 4 minutes a day reading at home, as opposed to 130 minutes a day watching TV. Yet reading is the basic skill on which all other school skills are built.

Although sports and other activities take up much of some students' time, television is the main competition for reading, so any campaign to get your child to read more will undoubtedly include turning off the TV for much of the evening.

There are also other ways that you can encourage a love of reading in your child. Probably the two most important ones are (1) to read to her when she is young and (2) to let her see that reading is an important part of your life. Once children begin to read on their own, even parents who have been conscientious about reading to them often believe their job is finished and that they can let their children take care of reading themselves. This is a mistake. Though your child can read, she still needs your encouragement to read. When she is a beginning reader, read with her. Even when she is a teenager, take her to the library or encourage her to go by herself. Also provide her with a wide variety of reading materials, including books and magazines aimed at her age level. Consider setting up a reading time each night during which all family members must spend twenty minutes or so reading. Many parents set reading time just before bedtime, and some even let children stay up later than usual if they are reading.

Take an interest in what your child reads. Discuss the books that each of you is reading and suggest that she try some you loved as a youngster, such as titles from the Bobbsey Twins series, Dr. Seuss books or *Charlotte's Web* by E. B. White. Look in particular for books on your child's favorite topics, which will make reading entertainment, not work. If your child is crazy about baseball, get sports stories and magazines. If she loves dinosaurs, select some of the many dinosaur books available. If your teenager dreams of owning a horse, ask the librarian to suggest horse stories. If you are going on a family vacation, look for books about the area you will be visiting, or about activities that you will be doing together. Don't worry if your child's interests run to subjects other than serious literature. It's better for her to read science fiction, romance stories or the comics than not to read at all.

Give your child books or magazine subscriptions as gifts. Encourage her to look up words in the dictionary or to consult the encyclopedia to learn about topics that interest her. Give her joke books or books of riddles. Ask your older child to read to her younger brother or sister. Look for TV shows based on books, or shows that would inspire your child to read about a particular subject or time period. Introduce your younger child to "Reading Rainbow," a public television series created in part by the National PTA that tells youngsters about exciting books. Your older child may find the news fascinating. If she recently has been hearing a lot about the war in Lebanon, look for books about the region. Check out a picture book on Russia before the next summit conference.

Try telling your young child stories. Even a child who finds reading boring will be intrigued if you tell the story of Cinderella or a ghost story. Then follow up with a book on fairy tales or the supernatural. Try to interest your child in writing as well. Give her a diary and ask her to write about her favorite activities. Encourage her to write a story, then make that story into a book and display it prominently in your house. Writing letters is also good practice, and many youngsters enjoy writing to a pen pal.

Be sure that your child isn't so busy with sports, a job or other activities that she doesn't have time to read. Praise her for her reading. You might even offer a reward if your child completes a certain number of books, especially during summer, when many young people get out of the habit of reading.

If your child seems to have special trouble reading, check

with your doctor about her eyesight and discuss with her teacher whether she might have learning disabilities. If you uncover no problems but still fail to get your child to read, keep trying. Young people go through phases. Even an avid reader may get involved in other activities and lose interest in books for a while. When your child reaches her next phase, she may find or rediscover the joys of books. So don't give up even if you don't see immediate results. Instead, persist in helping your child love to read, since this will help her in school and set her on the path to becoming a lifelong reader and learner.

Math and Science Really Matter

While most parents want their children to be good readers, fewer worry about whether they will excel in math and science. If you listen to a group of parents discussing their children's performance in school, you will likely hear comments such as the following: "I can't ever get my checkbook to balance, so it stands to reason that Billy isn't any good in math." "It's only boys who need science and math. Christie does well in English, French and social studies, so I don't worry about her lower grades in biology and algebra." "I hated math in school, and science wasn't much better. All we did was memorize stuff." "I tell Johnny not to waste time on math, since calculators and computers will do all the work for him when he grows up."

If you believe that math and science are not important, you are doing your child a disservice. Today math and science are more vital than ever before, but fewer and fewer American students are doing well in these subjects. When compared to students from other countries, American students perform more poorly in math and science than in other areas. Many foreign students study more complex levels of math and science and learn more than do American students. The fault for American students' poor showing lies both with schools and with parents.

Too many American schools and teachers fail to teach math and science effectively. They make math a difficult, repetitive and boring subject. For example, in many elementary schools math consists of six to eight years of computation drills. American schools devote too much time to teaching basic arithmetic—adding, subtracting, multiplying and dividing—and too little time to teaching problem solving through word problems, estimation, graphing, algebra and advanced math. Once students can do basic math, which they will probably do on a calculator or a computer anyway, they need to apply that knowledge to solve problems. A similar situation exists with respect to the teaching of science. Too many schools stress memorizing the periodic table of the elements, or the bones that comprise the skeleton, even though studies have shown that students learn science best through experimentation.

In addition, there is unfortunately still a strong feeling that math and science are male subjects—that boys are somehow naturally better at them than girls are, and that boys will have more use for them. Given today's career patterns, this is simply not true, yet parents, teachers and counselors are more likely to push boys than girls to study and do well in math and science. Thus, a bright girl thinking about what subjects to take in her senior year of high school is more likely to be advised to sign up for a social science or a humanities course rather than calculus or physics. Often parents don't even expect their daughters to excel in the science and math classes that they do take.

Since parents' attitudes are so important, you should examine your attitude toward math and science and be sure to recognize them for the important subjects that they are. "Continuing emphasis on these 'gateway' skills is important, since each course builds upon earlier ones," says Ann Kahn, a former National PTA president who works with the Mathematical Sciences Education Board. "Parents can help keep these gates open by encouraging students to take math seriously all during their school years. A closed gate greatly limits your children's choices, since it cuts off about 60 percent of possible college majors."

Parents can help their children do well in math and science by letting them know that they expect them to like and succeed in these subjects. They should tolerate nothing less than their children's best efforts. If your daughter is a good student, encourage her to take advanced math and science courses. Play mathematical games with your child—some card or board games are excellent for this purpose. Look for books about science in the library. Take your child for nature walks. Keep a careful check on her homework to see how she is doing in these subjects. Talk to her science and math teachers, the principal or the curriculum supervisors about how math and science are taught. If you believe that they are not being well taught in the school, ask your PTA president to call a meeting to see how instruction can be improved.

Talk to your child about how important math and science will be for workers in the twenty-first century. Technology has become a part of everyday life. Employers in every field are looking for workers who understand how to solve problems. Being illiterate in math and science today is almost as damaging as being unable to read.

Unplugging the TV

If you want your child to read and do well in school, you will likely have to limit TV watching. That doesn't mean that a child shouldn't watch any television. Rather, the amount should be restricted and care taken about what is watched. Be sure that you and your child don't automatically turn on TV when you get home and leave it on until bedtime, so that it is background noise in your home. Instead, select together what programs to watch. Then switch the TV on for the agreed-upon programs and off when they end. "Also keep a careful check on TV watching if your children are at home alone after school, since studies have found that many latchkey children spend most of their time alone watching TV and snacking," counsels Jean Dye, a Cleveland PTA leader who has been concerned about children and TV for more than two decades.

The amount of time most youngsters spend in front of the TV is appalling. By the time children graduate from high school, they may have spent fifteen thousand hours watching TV, as compared to eleven thousand in school. The average six- to eleven-year-old child watches twenty-five hours of TV a week, fifty-two weeks a year, which is more time than many children spend playing outside, going to school, studying, eating or doing anything besides sleeping.

Research has found that children who watch a lot of TV get lower grades, put less effort into schoolwork, have poorer reading skills, play less well with other children and have fewer hobbies and outside activities than do children who watch an hour or less of TV per day. Heavy watching has been linked to childhood obesity, since it keeps children from active play outside. Studies have also shown that watching violent TV can cause children to become less sensitive to the pain and suffering of others, more fearful of the world around them and more likely to behave aggressively.

The National PTA and Boys Town have developed suggestions for parents on how to stop TV from being a problem. Before you begin implementing those suggestions, chart the amount of time your family watches TV for one week so you will know how big a problem you have. Then several months later, make another chart to see your progress. Some researchers suggest that preschoolers watch no more than one hour of TV a day, and that students in elementary school watch less than two hours. Other experts would argue that even two hours a day is too much. You will have to determine the limit in your house.

Once you decide on the number of hours to be watched, select with your child at the start of the week what shows will be watched, and turn the TV on only for those shows. Set times when the TV must be off. For example, many household rules specify that there will be no TV during meals or until homework and instrument practice are finished. Determine how much TV can be watched on school nights and on weekends. If you have a videocassette recorder, tape programs that your child wants to see and show them at an allowed time, such as for half an hour or an hour after dinner.

Make a list of alternative activities that your child can do alone or that you can do as a family, such as riding a bicycle, painting a picture, working on macrame or model airplanes, learning magic tricks, playing games, having a friend over or even reading a book. Establish a "Family Game Night" or a time each week for art activities. If certain times are a special problem, such as Saturday mornings (when children want to camp out in front of the cartoons), see if you can schedule swimming lessons or playing catch to get them out of the house or involved in something besides TV.

"I would caution parents against allowing their children to have a TV set in their rooms," warns Jean Dye. "It is much better for TV watching to be a family activity than for children to sit alone in their rooms with only their TV for company." Also, as often as possible watch TV with your child. If she wants to see a show you aren't familiar with, watch an episode to be sure that it is something you want her to view. Consider carefully before letting your child watch violent shows. If a show you decide to watch includes shootings or beatings, talk about the violence. Explain that violence is faked on TV, but be sure your child realizes that real guns can kill and that other forms of violence can injure or kill as well. You might want to talk a little about how the families of victims must feel. Warn your child not to admire or glorify the bad guys. Also encourage her to watch programs in which characters find nonviolent means to solve their problems, and in which people are shown cooperating, helping and caring for others.

Talk about TV advertising with your child, too, because it is estimated that the average child sees about twenty thousand commercials a year. Since children under the age of six to eight can't distinguish between ads and programs, explain to them that the purpose of advertising is to sell products. This is particularly important, because deregulation of the television industry has opened the door for product-related shows—what some critics have called "program-length commercials"—whose aim is to convince children, via simple plots, that they can't live without the toys demonstrated. Tell your child which shows are really commercials. Also, even a very young child can be taught basic facts of nutrition, such as the need to limit sugar, so that she won't want to buy all the newest sugary cereals advertised.

Try to help your child become a critical TV viewer by asking her questions about what she is watching. Does she think the show is realistic? Would characters really act and talk that way? Ask her to suggest alternative endings for shows. Also point out that most people on TV are young, handsome and white. The "glamorous" jobs, like drug agent, attorney or surgeon, are usually held by men. Explain that women, older people and minorities are underrepresented on TV and often portrayed in narrow, stereotyped or negative ways. Ask your child to compare the people she knows or has studied about with those seen on TV.

On the positive side, you can use TV as a springboard for starting discussions with your child. For example, a news report on the drug-related death of a rock star or shows about problems like teen suicide can provide an opportunity for you to explain your beliefs and values, and to get your child talking about a sensitive subject.

"One final word of advice about TV," says Jean Dye. "Children learn by watching their parents. What will they learn as they see you watching TV?" Are you addicted to soap operas? Do you look forward to Friday nights so you can turn on the tube and space out? Do you use the TV as background noise for your daily life? Is every Sunday afternoon for months devoted to football? It is hard for parents to remember, but they are always setting examples for their children, even when sitting in front of the TV.

Underachievers

Underachievers are students who fail to live up to their potential, who do much more poorly in school than either their test scores would indicate or than their teachers and parents think they can. Although some children are recognized to be underachievers from a very young age, usually the problem shows up when they reach the third or fourth grade and begin to have their first serious homework assignments.

The first step to take if you or the teacher thinks that your child is an underachiever is to assess why she isn't doing better. You'll want to rule out any physical problems such as poor vision or hearing. You'll also want to talk to your child's teacher and possibly the school guidance counselor. Ask for a detailed explanation of the meaning of her test scores. Is there a large difference between what the tests predict that your child should be doing and her actual performance? If so, ask the teacher about possible causes of the problem.

If your child is in the early elementary years, don't be surprised if her teacher tells you not to worry, that you merely have a late bloomer. Experienced teachers know that students develop on their own schedule and that some learn to read or settle into the school routine later than others. So give your child time to start achieving instead of expecting her to be a star from the day she enters school. Also remember that some of the most creative and successful people in history, such as Albert Einstein and Winston Churchill, didn't do well early in their school careers.

Even if the teacher tells you that your child is just a late bloomer, be sure that she doesn't fall too far behind others in her class, since catching up can be difficult. Keep in close touch with her teacher. If your child has been in school for a couple of years and is still having trouble with reading, for example, ask the teacher if she should be tested for learning disabilities, since many underachievers have some problem that prevents their doing well. Ask what you can do at home to work with your child. Would more time reading together or a tutor help? Often "peer tutoring," help by other students of the same or approximate age, is effective. Is there a summer school program that over the vacation would prevent your child from losing newly learned skills? Does your child have low self-esteem or bad study habits? Work out a plan of action with the teacher to provide your child with the needed assistance. If you and the teacher aren't able to work out a way to help your child, talk to a counselor or the principal.

Remember that not all children can be at the top of their class. Maybe your child isn't an underachiever. Perhaps your expectations are unrealistically high. So while helping your child do her best in school, recognize her limitations as well. Parents who demand more than children can give put a tremendous amount of pressure on them and prepare them to fail.

PTAs in Action

Many PTAs conduct programs to help parents strengthen their children's self-esteem, to encourage students to enjoy reading, math and science, and to help them learn. The National PTA and the March of Dimes teamed up to develop a packet of material called "Parenting: The Underdeveloped Skill," which teaches parents how to be better communicators and how to foster self-esteem in their children. Ask your PTA president if this material can be used at parent education meetings. Following are examples of PTA programs to help parents help their children learn:

• The El Segundo Middle School PTA in El Segundo, California, organized "Parent Camp"—a day of workshops on topics such as building students' self-esteem, homework, college preparation and AIDS.

• The Rose Hill Junior High PTSA in Redmond, Washington, attempted to increase students' self-esteem by creating a Student of the Month program to reward six to ten children for leadership, exemplary behavior and an excellent attitude in school.

• The Butte View Elementary PTA in Butte View, Idaho, held a Student Appreciation Day for students who achieve in a variety of different activities.

• In the "Million Minutes of Reading Contest" sponsored by the Tiogue Elementary PTA in Coventry, Rhode Island, students read a total of 1,343,115 minutes in less than six months.

• The "B.E.A.R." (Be Excited About Reading) project of the White Oak Elementary PTA in White Oak, Pennsylvania, asked students to chart their daily reading. Certificates of achievement and pizzas were provided to participating children. The PTA also sponsored a workshop for parents on encouraging children to read.

• The Bay Village Council of PTAs in Bay Village, Ohio, also created a B.E.A.R. (Bay's Excited About Reading) program to encourage children and their parents to become better readers. Five local schools cooperated in the program, setting as a goal that every Bay Village resident read at least

6 books, for a total of 102,000 books, during the year. The goal was reached a month early.

• Happy Valley Elementary PTA members in Portland, Oregon, gave up their lunch hours to read to children at school.

• The Fernley Elementary School PTA in Fernley, Nevada, brought a dragon to school for the "Baggin' Dragon Reading Club." Children were given certificates and colorful dragon buttons, and a new scale was added to the dragon's body for every book the children read.

• The Neptune Beach Elementary PTA in Jacksonville, Florida, created a program called "Reading: The Road to Success." It turned the school hallways into roadways, with "fuel pumps" recording the number of pages the students read. School librarians became travel agents who "booked" passage to faraway lands. Demand for "fuel"—books—jumped 95 percent during the program.

• "Herbie Worm" was created by the Hoover PTA in Livonia, Michigan. Parents were sent a packet of information and recommendations for books to read to their children, and a piece was added to Herbie each time a book was read.

• "Project Bookworm," sponsored by the Dewey Elementary School PTA in Evanston, Illinois, placed special emphasis on helping low-achieving students and those with special needs to practice reading.

• The Washington PTA in North Platte, Nebraska, organized a "Prime Time Friday Night Read-a-thon" for fourth and fifth graders, who read and read during an overnight party.

• The Weyers Cave Elementary School PTA in Weyers Cave, Virginia, invited parents, grandparents, high school students, staff from the community library and members of the general public to school to read to students.

• The Irving School PTA in Dubuque, Iowa, set up and is currently staffing a "Writing Center."

• The Brockbank Junior High PTSA in Magna, Utah, created a "Lay Reader" program, in which thirty-seven volunteers were trained to help students with writing. Teachers in English classes assigned topics for students to write on, and readers worked directly with a few students, going over drafts of papers, strengthening style, giving positive feedback and helping with rewrites.

• Hundreds of book characters came to life in the "Books Alive" reading project of the Fairfield PTA Council in Fairfield, Connecticut. Each week for over two months, students in the Stratfield Elementary School recorded time spent reading either alone or with their parents as readers. Children gave oral readings at assemblies, and daily "guess-the-character" clues were read over the school's public-address system. The PTA decorated the school with large cardboard characters from books. Parents dressed up as book characters and visited the classrooms.

• At the Glendale Elementary School in Independence, Missouri, the PTA, principal and teachers created two special reading areas at school. One, an alcove next to the school library, was turned into a "Land of Oz," with murals, papier-mâché sculptures and comfortable chairs. The second—the Red Caboose, a real train caboose donated by the Missouri Pacific Railroad—was turned into a reading room. The PTA fitted out the caboose and PTA volunteers supervise it. PTA volunteers also staff the school library two days a week during the summer to encourage students to continue reading.

• The Downers Grove Area PTA Council in Downers Grove, Illinois, two of the suburb's school districts and the Downers Grove Public Library sponsor the Downers Grove Children's Author Festival. As many as thirty-four Chicago-area authors and artists are invited to visit classrooms and talk to the students during the week-long festival.

• When the Weber Council PTA in Ogden, Utah, decided to sponsor a "Junior Authors' Fair," it asked all students to write a book on any topic that interested them. The books were compiled and bound by parents and teachers, and displayed at the fair. In addition, published authors were invited to attend and to talk with the junior authors.

• The Mt. Park Elementary PTA in Roswell, Georgia, created the Mustang Publishing Company to "publish" a book by each child in the school. Parent volunteers and school staff encouraged children to write. Then parents worked with the authors on copy and hand-bound the books.

• PTA members at two Illinois schools recently cooperated with their teachers to sponsor a "No TV Day." The Bert Fulton School and Helen B. Sandidge School PTA in Tinley Park read an article about the effects of television on children in *PTA Today*. PTA leaders asked parents to pledge not to watch TV or to allow their children to watch for one day. Students made posters encouraging participation, and teachers set up demonstrations in their classrooms of games, puzzles, hobbies and other activities that families could do. A hotline with suggestions for family activities was also put into operation. At least one hundred families turned off their TVs for the day.

• When the Ligonier Valley PTA in Ligonier, Pennsylvania, learned that 67 percent of its elementary school students watched three or more hours of TV nightly, it created a "Watch Less TV Project." PTA members developed a reading list and a list of alternative activities for families. Students were asked to record the number of hours they watched TV for a week and then to agree with their parents on a daily limit. Those students who did not exceed their limit were honored each day.

• The Roosevelt Elementary PTA in Fargo, North Dakota, wanted to give children more computer time than they were receiving, so it sponsored the Roosevelt Computer Club to teach students basic computer skills as well as higher-level problem-solving abilities. Parents currently volunteer to work with the students.

• PTA members at School One in Scotch Plains-Fanwood,

New Jersey, run a lunchtime computer program for students in the second, third and fourth grades. A training session was held initially to acquaint parents with the computer and software.

• Recognizing that many parents are uncomfortable with math and science, the Winston Churchill PTA in Palatine, Illinois, held a "Family Night in Science" for students and their parents.

• The Almance Elementary PTA in Giboro, North Carolina, combined two disciplines, sponsoring an Art/Science Fair to encourage student participation in both subjects and to show parents what their children were doing in these areas.

• The Clarkmoor PTA in Ft. Lewis, Washington, staged "Passport to Discovery," a science carnival for families. Booths were set up where students and their parents could "Dig Those Bones" (assemble a model dinosaur) or learn about computers. Children's science projects were also displayed.

• The Twin Lakes PTA in Federal Way, Washington, declared "Science Month." Activities included a program for parents on "Creative Thinking in Science," a "Scientists-in-Residence Program" (with twenty-eight different scientists visiting classrooms), a science fair and science exhibits such as moon rocks.

• The Crabapple Middle School PTA in Roswell, Georgia, provided a study skills workshop.

• The Evergreen Junior High PTSA in Redmond, Washington, held a parent/student homework workshop.

• The Petaluma Senior High School PTSA in Petaluma, California, staffed a study hall at school and helped students with homework assignments.

• Many PTAs have organized programs to alert parents if their children skip school or if they fail to arrive at school safely. For example, the Stone School PTA in Saginaw, Michigan, sponsors a "Callers on Absenteeism Program." In many such programs the PTA schedules parents to telephone the parents of students who are absent.

• The R. D. Head Elementary PTA in Lilburn, Georgia, attacks the absenteeism problem from a different angle. It encourages attendance by many means, including setting up competitions between classes to see which has the highest attendance. Attendance at the school has increased and now exceeds the average for all schools in the county.

CHAPTER

6

The Out-of-School Hours

EMMA, WHO IS five, walks home from kindergarten each day with her eleven-year-old brother, Matthew, who uses his key to let them into their house. Matthew calls their mother at work to tell her they arrived safely. Next, he gives Emma a bag of cookies and a soda and turns on the TV in the living room for her. He then takes his own snack into the bedroom and watches his favorite television shows. Their dad usually arrives home about six o'clock to find Emma dozing on the couch and Matthew glued to the latest superhero episode.

Ben, who is thirteen, is picked up from school by his mother or father, who whisks him off to soccer, hockey or baseball practice, or to his scout meeting, piano lesson or karate class. Saturdays in his family are filled with more practices and games (of whichever sport is in season), swimming meets, computer classes, and attempts to fit in piano practice and an extra session with his Spanish tutor.

Amy participates in sports and takes ballet lessons, but she has lots of free time for play and just "hanging out" however a nine-year-old thinks best. "We don't want to push her too hard," says her mother. "We like for her to be outside playing with friends or doing her homework, reading and enjoying herself at home most of the time."

These four children have very different lives. Which schedule most closely resembles your child's?

Once children's out-of-school hours were viewed as time to play. Today many children work harder when they aren't in school than when they are. They pack the after-school hours, evenings and weekends with lessons, scouting, sports, jobs, extracurricular activities, homework, household chores and family responsibilities. Many parents view the out-of-school hours as critical to their children's success in school and life, pushing them to achieve at the gymnasium, the ball diamond and the music practice hall. Other youngsters are forced from an early age to take responsibility for both themselves and often for younger brothers and sisters while their parents are at work. Many of these children spend their time watching TV, snacking and filling as best they can the long, boring hours until their parents arrive.

"While everyone recognizes that the out-of-school hours should not be wasted, I hope that children still have time to play and to have a cookie," comments Anne Campbell, retired commissioner of education for Nebraska and a member of the National PTA board of directors. "Play is critically important in helping children learn to get along with other children and in developing self-esteem. It's a way for youngsters to get to know themselves, to explore and develop their curiosity."

Karen Bauer, an early childhood educator at Villa Maria College, in Erie, Pennsylvania, wrote in *PTA Today* that "play has been called 'children's work.' . . . It provides children with a means to integrate their experiences and to understand a complex world." She says many parents believe their children should be doing something more productive than merely having fun. But actually, play fosters physical, emotional, intellectual and social development. Therefore, encourage your child to play, because it is vital for his development as well as his happiness.

A somewhat different view is taken by Joan Bergstrom, a professor of early childhood studies at Wheelock College in Boston and the author of *School's Out—Now What?* Bergstrom advises parents not to let their children's time slip away, especially if they are six to twelve years old. She suggests that parents help plan their children's schedule so that three to six, or even seven hours a week are spent in organized activities.

Bergstrom advises parents to observe their children, talk with them about their interests and then decide together on activities that truly appeal to them, and for which the family has time and money. She writes in *PTA Today,* "Some people feel that when adults help children plan their out-of-school time, they are being 'pushy.' This need not be true; parents can learn to strike a delicate balance between demanding too much and providing too little." But like Campbell and Bauer, Bergstrom warns that children need time for play. "Play provides opportunities for a child to develop and perfect skills, to solve problems and to be in control. Every child needs time to tell jokes, play tricks and to just act silly."

David Elkind writes in *The Hurried Child,* "The pressure to grow up fast, to achieve early in the area of sports, academics and social interaction, is very great in middle class America. Children have to achieve success early or they are regarded as losers." Elkind is especially concerned about young children who are pushed into competitive sports by parents who are living out their own dreams through their children. "Generally it is parent need, not a child's authentic wish, that pushes children into team sports at an early age. School-age children need the opportunity to play their own games, make up their own rules, abide by their own timetable. . . . Certainly children learn something from competitive sports—for example, competence, self-assurance, teamwork. But . . . many end up feeling like failures."

It isn't just an overemphasis on team sports that concerns

Elkind. He warns parents against too many organized, highly structured activities and advises them not to push children too early into clubs, computers, music, or swimming, skiing or ballet lessons. Elkind believes that many children who are pushed too quickly by parents, the media and schools suffer negative consequences by the time they reach adolescence, such as experimentation with drugs, alcohol and sex, stress-induced diseases, crime and other antisocial behavior, and suicide.

Decide what activities you want your young child to participate in. Keep in mind his abilities, age and interests. Also be sure that potential coaches or teachers stress fun and learning. Do they build self-esteem by helping children to succeed and by allowing all young children to play rather than concentrate solely on winning?

As your child grows older, you will have less influence over what he does and does not participate in. Still, you will probably discover times when it will be necessary to encourage your child to continue with lessons as his interest wanes, and to push him to get out of the house to make new friends or try new activities, or to convince him that he is undertaking too much.

Kids with Keys, Parents with Jobs

In 1987, a Metropolitan Life/Harris poll of American teachers found that teachers believed the number one cause of students' difficulty in school was their being left at home alone before and after school. The same poll found that 41 percent of parents said that their children were often on their own after school. Estimates of the number of children at home alone each day vary from 2 million to 7 million. No one knows exactly how many children fall into this category, but everyone agrees that the number is large and that these latchkey children are found in every community, and in every social and economic class in America.

Do parents leave their children alone because they can't afford other care or have no other choice? While in many cases this is undoubtedly true, studies (including a recent report by the U.S. Census Bureau) have found that white, middle-class, suburban families are more likely to have latchkey children than are poor, black, urban dwellers. Better educated, more affluent parents living in relatively safe communities, especially well-educated mothers with white-collar jobs, seem more likely to believe their children are mature enough to take care of themselves.

"Many child-care experts advise against leaving children under the age of twelve on their own for long periods of time," reports Denise Carter, director of programs at the National PTA. Studies have shown that some latchkey children feel fearful, lonely or bored at home alone, while others show a decrease in social skills and in self-esteem. On the other hand, some children like being on their own and relish their independence.

Every child is different, so parents must carefully consider their own child's needs, personality and level of maturity when deciding on child-care arrangements. "It is clear, though, that young children need supervision. Even when they reach ten or twelve years old, you should do everything possible to make some arrangement so that you don't have to leave your children at home alone if you have the slightest doubt that they are capable of taking care of themselves, or if your children are hesitant about staying by themselves," Carter recommends.

Before deciding to leave your child alone, you should explore all the child-care options available, including family day-care providers who look after children in their homes, school-age child-care programs, day-care centers, baby-sitters who come to parents' homes, and help from friends and relatives. Ask your friends whom they use. Your local schools, the PTA, social service groups, or the YMCA and YWCA may have compiled child-care resource lists.

A number of schools and social service groups run supervised programs for school-age children. Because few jobs coincide with the schedule for school holidays or teacher inservice days, many of these groups provide care on no-school days and even during summer vacation, as well as before and after school. A 1988 study by the National Association of Elementary School Principals found, though, that there is a vast gap between the supply and demand for before-school and after-school programs. Also, while 84 percent of elementary and middle school principals surveyed said that they believe children in their communities need supervision during out-of-school hours, only 22 percent of their schools offer such care.

If your school or another group in your community doesn't offer school-age child care, ask your PTA president to call a meeting to discuss whether such a program is needed. You and other parents may want to work through your PTA or another group, such as a local community center or the Y to start a program. Often community groups will join with the schools to provide care. In other cases, schools have been convinced to take over such programs once they have been started by the PTA or another group.

If there is no child-care program and no possibility of getting one started quickly in your area, and if good child care isn't available, you may consider allowing your preteen child to stay at home alone for short periods each day. "But think very, very carefully about your children's safety and well-being, including what effect being alone will have on them before deciding to leave them alone," Carter stresses. "It is always safer and better for children to have adult supervision, so be sure that there is an adult to check on them and that they are really old enough to be left alone."

Parents should find out their children's true feelings before deciding to allow them to be unsupervised. Hold an ongoing dialogue, since some children feel guilty about ad-

CHILD-CARE OPTIONS

- Find out if your local school, Y, PTA, community center or place of worship offers school-age child-care programs or after-school activities for children. Don't overlook day-care centers, some of which care for children before and after school and arrange for transportation between school and the center.
- Ask if your school, community center or PTA can begin such a program or sponsor after-school activities if none exist.
- Enlist the help of grandparents or other close relatives.
- See if a neighborhood parent provides family day care for children before and after school.
- Hire a baby-sitter to come to your home. A sitter should be mature, have good references and relate well to children.
- Talk to your employer. A few companies offer on-site or off-site child-care centers for employees' children. Other companies offer referral services and child-care expense benefits. Ask if such services can be started at your place of work, or whether a flex-time schedule can be instituted so that you can be home with your child after school.
- Learn about any child-care referral services in your area. If none exist, discuss starting one with your Y, PTA or other community service organizations.

mitting they are scared. Instead of asking your child if he is afraid of being left alone, ask indirect questions such as, "Do you feel uncomfortable if someone knocks on the door when you're alone?" "Are you afraid of being at home alone after dark?" "Are you nervous when the phone rings?" "What do you do when you hear strange noises?" "What do you think you'd like to do if you were home alone?" Your child's responses can provide clues to his fears and anxieties that can help you decide if he is ready to be left alone.

Safety training is essential for all children whether they are going to be by themselves or not, since even the best-laid plans can sometimes go wrong. Help your child decide how to respond to these situations: the lights go off; his brother doesn't arrive home on schedule; his sister is injured at home; a kitchen appliance begins to sizzle and smoke; you call to say that you have missed your train and will be two hours late; an adult you know asks to come into the house to borrow a tool; a plumber knocks on the door and says that a pipe is leaking. Remember to teach safety rules in a nonthreatening way. Your goal should be to show your child how to stay safe. This will enhance his self-esteem and help him recognize his ability to handle potentially serious problems. The more confidence he has, the better prepared he

A SAFETY CHECKLIST FOR CHILDREN HOME ALONE

All children, not just latchkey children, need to know:

- Their full name, address and phone number (including area code).
- Their parents' names, and the names and phone numbers of their employers.
- Emergency phone numbers such as fire, police, doctor and at least two adults to call in case they can't reach you in an emergency.
- How to carry a key so that it is secure but out of sight. It may hang from a necklace worn inside clothing or be safety-pinned inside a pant or dress pocket.
- Never to enter the house if a door is ajar, a window is broken or anything looks odd. Children should know to go to a neighbor or to a pay phone to call you or the police.
- What to do if they think they're being followed or if a stranger tries to approach them. Tell your child to run to a "block home" or to the nearby house of a friend where he knows someone will be home. He can also run into a local office or store and tell the proprietor.
- That they should avoid walking home alone or playing alone on the way home from school.

❦ ❦ ❦

will be to cope with any crisis, and the fewer mishaps he will have.

If children are to be left alone, they must have developed the judgment necessary to turn off the television and begin their homework, or to say no to friends who encourage them to do something dangerous. They should know that at all times they must abide by such house rules as not to use the stove, to let anyone into the house or to have friends over without advance approval from their parents. Remember, too, that if children are allowed to help make these rules, they will be more likely to follow them.

- How to answer the telephone without letting callers know they are alone. Help your child decide upon a response, such as "My mom is busy and can't come to the phone right now. May I take a message?" If a caller continues to ask for a parent or wants to know if he is alone, your child should hang up the phone.
- To call a check-in person (parent, grandparent, neighbor or friend) at a set time each day.
- How to respond to a knock at the door. Decide ahead of time whether you want your child to ignore knocks or to say, for example, "I can't help you now."
- What to do if they miss the school bus or their ride to or from school.
- What to do if there's bad weather such as a thunderstorm, blizzard or tornado warning. Children might be told to stay at school or to call a parent or a taxi, or you may want to arrange for a friend or neighbor to pick up your child if weather conditions deteriorate.
- How to get out of the house quickly and safely in case of a fire. This includes knowing not to report a fire from their home phone, since getting out of the house is the first priority.
- How to respond to other types of emergencies, and general safety rules at home.
- How to use their hours at home productively, as well as how to have fun by themselves.

To provide additional support, you should see if your community offers backup services such as "block home" or "block parent" programs. These are safe people or houses to which children can go if they feel threatened. Telephone hotlines or "warmlines" may also be helpful, since they allow children to call and talk to someone if they are frightened or lonely or just need to talk. But these are merely support services, not answers to the question of whether your child is safe and comfortable at home alone. You are going to have to decide the answer to that hard question based on your knowledge of your child and your community. The decision about how your child is cared for out of school may well be the most important decision you make as a working parent. So think about it long and carefully, and be sure that both you and your child are satisfied with what you decide.

Sports and Extracurricular Activities

Extracurricular activities give students an opportunity for fun, recognition and success; a chance to develop physical, social and intellectual abilities; and a way to round out their education. Also, extracurricular activities can help students gain admission to a college, since many weigh extracurricular activities along with grades and test scores. Some studies have even suggested that extracurricular activities may increase students' sense of identification with school to such an extent that the activities help prevent students from dropping out. Yet less than half of all students participate in extracurricular activities. Students who attend suburban schools or smaller schools with an enrollment under fifteen hundred are most likely to participate in extracurricular activities, as are white, college-bound, middle-class and academically successful boys.

Sports are clearly the most popular extracurricular activity in most schools. In fact, some critics charge that sports receive too much attention and money in many schools and that student athletes don't have enough time to attend classes and do homework. Still, sports provide millions of boys and girls with much-needed physical exercise and allow them to develop skills and competence, to be good at something, to learn to work together with others and to enhance their self-esteem. Sports are also fun, and many young children make new friends on the tennis courts or the soccer field.

But sports and especially the competition of team sports can place heavy pressure on young people. For those who fail to live up to the expectations of their parents, their coach or themselves, athletics can lead to disappointment and loss of self-esteem. Some parents want their children to participate in sports because they think that sports build character and give children an incentive to work hard in school. Other parents hesitate about allowing their children to participate in sports because they fear that athletics will divert them from school work, thus lowering grades and achievement.

The effect that participation in athletics has on your child will depend on his personality, academic ability and study habits, though research seems to suggest that such participation slightly decreases the average boy's grades and academic achievement. At the same time participation increases his educational aspirations and helps keep him from dropping out of school or getting into trouble with the law. Sports may even help him in his later career, since one study found that fifteen years after graduation, men who had been high school athletes had higher career aspirations and a higher income than did nonathletes. Also, athletics provide high school boys with a visibility that makes it easier for them to become school leaders, which in turn increases their likelihood of going on to college.

Girls need physical fitness as much as boys do, and they benefit from the experience of cooperating and the increase in self-esteem that sports can provide. Girls get an extra benefit from certain sports, since activities such as running or hiking build stronger bones, which may prevent them in later years from developing osteoporosis, a condition that makes bones brittle. We don't know, though, what effect athletics have on girls' academic performance or on their aspirations, since few studies have been done in this area.

In judging whether your child should participate in sports or how much time and attention he should give to athletic endeavors, consider his interests and abilities, his activity level, how he normally spends his time (will sports take too much time away from other activities, including schoolwork), the available sports, the philosophy and skills of the potential coaches and how careful coaches are to ensure players' safety and emotional well-being.

Many experts advise that very young children spend their time trying out different sports and developing general skills rather than concentrating on one or two sports. Many of the same experts advise that even older children and teens refrain from participating in team sports all year long. It's your job to help your child choose carefully which extracurricular activities he will be involved in, to keep sports or other activities in perspective and to monitor his academic progress so that grades and learning don't suffer as a consequence of extracurricular activities.

Teens with Jobs

Many parents encourage their high school children to work part-time because they believe that working teaches responsibility and the value of money, offers a preview of the world of work, lets them learn a little about various jobs and careers, and allows them to earn money to save for college or to help pay for clothes and recreation. Besides, many parents say, "I worked and so should my kids." But in recent years the pattern of teen work has changed, and along with that change have come questions about whether the way many teens are working is good or bad.

Teens' working has become the norm. A national survey found that about 60 percent of high school sophomores and 75 percent of seniors were working. Many of these teens work long hours rather than just a few afternoons or evenings a week. One fourth of all high school sophomores work half-time, and 10 percent of seniors have a work week equal to a full-time job.

Most teens work not to help their families with expenses or to save for college but to afford clothes, stereos and cars. According to Ellen Greenberger, who has studied teenage work patterns, only about 20 percent of those who work contribute to family expenses, and few save money despite the fact that the average working teen earns between $200 and $300 a month. In part because of a lack of jobs in the inner city, poor and black teens are less likely to work than are white, middle-class students, who need the money less.

Greenberger and Laurence Steinberg, authors of *When Teenagers Work,* found that working teens may enjoy such benefits as improved work habits, increased self-reliance (especially on the part of girls) and the ability to command higher wages right after graduation. They also discovered that if the work hours are too long, teens may experience an increased use of alcohol and drugs, a greater chance of dropping out of school, a lack of interest in school and a lessening of the time spent on schoolwork. For this reason, the authors suggest that teens limit the weekly work hours during the school year to fifteen for sophomores and twenty for seniors. It is particularly important, they believe, that teens not work long hours during the afternoons and evenings of school days. They also suggest that students look for more interesting jobs if their work becomes routine and boring. Finally, they suggest that if money is not a factor, the teens consider pursuing traditional extracurricular activities or community service instead.

If your teen works, monitor his weekly hours of employment and determine whether work is taking time away from homework or other important activities. For example, is your child dropping out of the French club or band to spend four hours an evening wrapping hamburgers? Is he learning anything from his job or making the kind of friends that you want him to have? Think carefully about what will help him most in the long run and remember that, as Greenberger says, "A student's real job is going to school."

PTAs in Action

Here are examples of PTAs that help children during their out-of-school hours:

- Because of its concern for the hundreds of thousands of latchkey children in the Los Angeles area, the Thirty-first District PTSA decided to set up school-age child-care programs in the San Fernando Valley area in 1982. With assistance from the Los Angeles Unified School District, PTSA leaders hired program directors, set up facilities, and opened before- and after-school programs for 150 students in five schools. By 1988, the programs had expanded to thirteen schools, serving more than 730 students with a paid staff of 67. Full and partial scholarships are available for students whose parents cannot afford the modest fee for the Thirty-first District PTSA latchkey projects.
- For more than forty years the Elmhurst PTA Council in Elmhurst, Illinois, has sponsored the Elmhurst Children's Theatre, which presents three plays a year starring children from its community. Rehearsals and other activities have helped fill the out-of-school hours for thousands of Elmhurst's young people.
- Since 1973 the Third Street School PTA in Los Angeles has sponsored "Superschool," an enrichment program for students. Each year fifteen to twenty classes are offered in subjects such as film animation, miniature-house building,

foreign languages, computers, chess, roller skating, astronomy, calligraphy and various aspects of dance, drama, music and art. Nearly 50 percent of the students in the school attend, paying twenty to fifty dollars for a class lasting from twelve to sixteen weeks. Fee waivers are available for students from needy families. The PTA hires teachers from the California School of Music and the California Institute for the Arts as well as recruits parents with expertise.

- The Spotswood Elementary School PTA in Fredericksburg, Virginia, asks parents and community members to volunteer their talents to teach classes in photography, science, storytelling, cross-stitch, aerobics, French, Spanish, chess and checkers, among other topics.
- The Mohawk Elementary School PTA in Springfield, Oregon, offered a four-week series of classes entitled "Castles, Costumes and Flying Machines." More than fifty parent volunteers taught students about life in the Middle Ages. The PTA also sponsored a medieval fair, a costume contest and an outdoor feast.
- The Greensboro Council of PTAs in Greensboro, North Carolina, sponsors a "Saturday Enrichment Program" and provides scholarships for those children in need of financial support.
- The Greenwood Elementary PTA in Des Moines, Iowa, sponsored a week of minicourses for students. Subjects covered included golf, bicycle safety, dog obedience, stamp collecting and ice-cream making. The Greenwood Elementary PTA also enlisted one thousand volunteers to build a children's playground at their school. Funding was provided by the community, school alumni, foundations and local corporations. The volunteers worked with a local architect, whose services were free of charge. After many weeks of preliminary work, the playground was constructed in just four days.
- The Shawnee Mission East PTA in Shawnee Mission, Kan-

sas, encourages students to spend their out-of-school time working as community volunteers. It created a video telling students how to become clowns in hospitals and help handicapped children and the elderly, among other activities. Students who perform forty-five hours of community service get a notation on their high school transcript.

CHAPTER

7

The Needs of the Special Child

YOU MAY LEARN that your child is handicapped shortly after birth. Or later you may notice that she doesn't seem to hear noises or learn as quickly as other children her age. On the other hand, you may discover you have a gifted child when she teaches herself to read in preschool, or at age three starts picking out tunes on your piano. Or, you may first become aware of her special needs—either because she is handicapped *or* gifted—when you receive a note from her teacher advising you that the school would like to test your daughter to see if she has a learning disability, or to determine if she would benefit from special programs for the gifted.

However and whenever you become aware of your child's special needs, your priority should be to learn what can be done to fill those needs. One of the first places you should turn for help is your local public school, where special teachers and programs may be available to help your child make the most of her talents and abilities.

"Until the 1970s many children with special needs received little education in their local public schools," says Freda Thorlaksson, a longtime PTA leader from Chico, California. Retarded children were sometimes sent to special schools or allowed to attend early elementary grades. Few accommodations, though, were made to help them learn, and many retarded children received no schooling at all. Physically handicapped children who needed special assistance also found little welcome at most public schools. Children with emotional problems that caused them to be disruptive or unable to follow regular class rules were frequently expelled. Most schools didn't have the desire, and teachers didn't have the training, to teach students who were somehow different.

At the other end of the spectrum, the very bright students—those who would today be called gifted and talented—were left on their own. "Now and then there was a teacher who took special interest in the brightest students and tried to adapt teaching methods and curriculum to serve them, but that was the exception rather than the rule," says Thorlaksson.

In the 1970s a few states passed laws requiring special education services for handicapped students, and federal court cases forced schools in a number of states to increase services. Then Congress passed the Rehabilitation Act of 1973, which outlawed discrimination based on handicaps and said that institutions receiving federal funds must provide the same services to the handicapped. Two years later Congress passed the Education for All Handicapped Children Act of 1975 (commonly known as Public Law 94-142, or PL 94-142), which required public schools to provide educational programs for hundreds of thousands of handicapped children. The National PTA worked long and hard for passage of PL 94-142 and continues to support adequate funding for this vital legislation.

Public Law 94-142 has been called the handicapped students' bill of rights because it requires public schools to provide them with a "free, appropriate public education" in the least restrictive environment possible, along with such related services as (1) early identification and assessment of handicaps, (2) speech and hearing therapy, (3) physical and occupational therapy, (4) counseling, (5) diagnostic medical services and (6) transportation to and from school or any other facility to receive services. PL 94-142 also dramatically increased the amount of federal money for aid to special students, although the dollars—which have never approached the actual amount needed to provide for all these services—have been declining in recent years. Even if federal funds are not forthcoming, states are required to see that special children receive the mandated education. In practice, this has meant that states have had to pick up much of the cost of special education.

Amendments have changed the rules and regulations that implement PL 94-142 somewhat over the years, but the basic policy remains the same. Children between the ages of three and twenty-one are to be provided with an education and related services. Some federal funds are available to provide services to children from birth, and some states continue services until age twenty-six. All children needing services are eligible for special education whether they attend public or private schools or are homebound, hospitalized or in another institution.

The law requires that students be placed in the "least restrictive environment," and that efforts must be made to place handicapped students in regular schools and regular classrooms, and to move students out of special education and into regular education as soon as possible. This is called mainstreaming. Parents must be continually involved in the special education process and must give their consent at various stages, for example before children can be tested or before they can receive special services.

If your child has a problem, handicap or special need, you will want to learn all you can about the condition and your child's rights. Check your local library to see if books listed in the Additional Readings section or similar books are available, or if they can be obtained through an interlibrary loan. Contact your state department of education and any of the national advocacy and support associations that serve families of persons with your child's handicap. Ask the reference librarian at your local public library to help you find the names and addresses of other associations.

The Special Education System

All school districts and state education departments are required by federal law to seek out the children in their community or state who need special services before they begin school. Your school may offer free screening for children with suspected handicaps. Your doctor or a social service agency may refer you to your local public school district, or you may contact your school district directly and ask for an evaluation of your child. If your child is already in school, you may receive a call or letter telling you that her teacher has suggested an evaluation to see if special education would be appropriate.

PL 94-142 requires that special education services be provided for children who are mentally retarded (with low IQ and trouble adapting to regular environments), are hearing- or vision-impaired, are physically handicapped (as long as their disability interferes with their ability to learn in a regular classroom), suffer from communication disorders (such as having difficulty in speaking or understanding spoken language), have emotional or behavioral problems that interfere with their education, or who have a wide variety of learning disabilities that prevent them from learning as much as their intellectual abilities would seemingly allow. All of these children are eligible because they are educationally handicapped. A physical handicap or another condition that does not interfere with the ability to learn in regular classrooms does not qualify children for special education. Also, not all students who have trouble learning or who do poorly in school

ASSOCIATIONS SERVING CHILDREN WITH SPECIAL NEEDS

Council for Exceptional Children (both handicapped and gifted)
1920 Association Drive
Reston, VA 22091

Association for Children and Adults with Learning Disabilities
4156 Library Road
Pittsburgh, PA 15234

Association for Retarded Citizens of the United States
P.O. Box 6109
Arlington, TX 76005

National Easter Seal Society
2023 W. Ogden Avenue
Chicago, IL 60612

National Federation of the Blind
1800 Johnson Street
Baltimore, MD 21230

National Handicapped Sports and Recreation Association
1145 19th Street NW
Washington, DC 20036

Special Olympics
1701 K Street NW
Washington, DC 20006

necessarily qualify. They are eligible only if there is a disabling condition present that makes it difficult for them to learn without special help.

Before your child can be evaluated for special education, you must give your written consent. But first ask why it is thought necessary, what the evaluation will consist of, and when it will be given. In addition, ask for a copy of the school district's special education policies and procedures. So that you can provide useful information about your child, review her behavior and medical history, think about how she learns best, and check her baby book to see when she achieved such developmental milestones as walking and talking.

The evaluation will be conducted free of charge by a team of school staff and will include a variety of individually administered tests. After all the tests are concluded and other information has been gathered, there will be a meeting to determine the student's eligibility for special education services. Some school districts automatically invite parents to participate in these meetings, while other districts don't. Ask in advance to attend the eligibility meeting. Most districts will allow it.

At the eligibility meeting, special education specialists from the school district and representatives from your local school will review the evaluation's findings to decide whether your child is eligible for special services. In most states, if your child is declared eligible, the participants will classify the handicap. Thus, for example, they may decide that your child is mentally or visually handicapped and authorize services for the conditions specified. The school must inform you of the results of the evaluation, and you can request an independent or private evaluation if you disagree. You can also appeal the eligibility decision and ask for a review. If after the review you are still not satisfied, you can ask for an impartial hearing.

Once your child is declared eligible for special education, you will be asked to participate in a meeting to develop an individualized education program (IEP) for your child. Be sure to attend this vital meeting. You will have to give written consent to this document before the program is put into effect. The IEP will include your child's placement, meaning where your child will be educated. This may be in the regular classroom, with special assistance provided in the classroom. It may be in the regular classroom, but with certain periods spent each day in a "resource room" with a special education teacher. It may be primarily in a "self contained" classroom with other similarly handicapped children, with mainstreaming at certain times each day (such as for physical education class and lunch hour with nonhandicapped students). It may be entirely with handicapped students in a self-contained classroom, or in a separate school or at your home or in a hospital or other institution.

Pay careful attention to the development of the IEP, since it will set the course of your child's education for at least the rest of the school year. You should insist that the IEP have clearly stated, understandable and measurable goals and objectives. For example, depending on your child's age, status and handicap, a goal might be for your child to learn to say, recognize and write her ABC's by the end of the school year. The objectives might be for her to recite the alphabet by January 1, recognize the alphabet by March 1 and print the alphabet in capital letters by June 15. Make sure the IEP spells out all the related services that your child will receive, such as speech therapy for half an hour, twice a week; occupational therapy for fifty minutes, three times a week; counseling for an hour, once a week; and transportation arrangements to and from school, since only those services listed in the IEP will be provided. It should also list any special equipment, such as a tape recorder, that will help your child learn or adapt to classes.

Before signing the plan, you may want to visit the classes or school that your child would attend and talk to the special education teachers or discuss the IEP with a knowledgeable parent whose child has gone through special education. If you have major disagreements with the IEP, you can ask that the school change it. If this isn't done to your satisfaction, you can ask for a hearing before an impartial hearing officer. If you are still not satisfied, you may want to file a complaint with your state department of education or the U.S. Education Department's Office for Civil Rights. Ultimately you may have to sue the school system to try to get the services your child needs. More likely, though, you and the school will be able to work out disagreements informally.

Once you sign the IEP, it will be put into effect and your child will begin receiving the services in the agreed-upon location. The school must review the IEP at least once a year to ascertain that it is being effectively carried out, or you can ask for a review sooner than that. At no time may your child's placement or the IEP be changed or terminated without your written consent. All special education students must be completely reevaluated at least every three years. At that time there will be a new eligibility meeting. If your child is still eligible, you will be asked to participate in a meeting to draw up a new IEP and to give your written consent to it.

Your job is not finished once your child begins to receive special education services. Instead, you should carefully monitor progress, assure yourself that the IEP is being carried out, work closely with teachers to see how your child is doing and learn what you can do at home to reinforce the work at school. Discuss with the teachers whether you should schedule regular monthly meetings or rely on phone calls and notes. Some parents and special education teachers exchange notes each day outlining activities undertaken at school and what is happening at home.

Problems with Special Education

Most schools have adapted fairly well to the changes resulting from PL 94-142 and are making real efforts to provide services for the more than 4.6 million children needing special help. However, problems remain. Often money is scarce. This means that some handicapped children are never identified and receive no help, while others receive less than they need. Educating the handicapped is expensive, averaging about twice as much as educating nonhandicapped students. While studies show that this is money well spent, because the education and other services save much more money in the long run than they cost, there is never enough money. Frequently there aren't enough well-trained special education teachers, either.

Another problem is that special education places a stigma on handicapped students. Nonhandicapped students sometimes call special education classes "dummy classes." Sometimes even teachers, administrators and parents cease to view handicapped children as individuals, referring to them as LD (learning disabled) or EMH (educable mentally handicapped) or some other name, rather than Suzy and Johnny. Labels have a strong tendency to remain with students, making it difficult for those who no longer need special education services to be accepted by other students or regular teachers.

Minorities are greatly overrepresented in the ranks of special education students. This has given rise to charges that the minority children who have problems learning or adapting to the school routine are being shipped off to special education classes rather than worked with in the regular classroom.

Another potential problem concerns discipline. Special students often present teachers with exceedingly difficult discipline problems. How, for example, do you make a child with severe emotional problems conform to school rules? PL 94-142 says that handicapped children may not be disciplined for actions or behavior that results from their handicapping condition. Thus, hyperactive children cannot be punished for their inability to sit still during class, and teachers have to find other ways of dealing with this behavior. They often use a technique called behavior modification, in which students are rewarded for good behavior and denied privileges if their behavior is bad. All parents and teachers use behavior modification to some extent, but these techniques can be overused or used improperly when dealing with handicapped students. You may want to ask that discipline plans be written into the IEP, and be sure that you understand and agree with all discipline methods.

Likewise, you will want to think carefully about any medication that is prescribed to help your child learn. Schools cannot prescribe medication, and no medicine can be given without parents' consent, but your family doctor or the doctor doing medical tests as part of your child's special education evaluation may suggest medicine. Before agreeing to give your child any medication, discuss carefully with the doctor why the medicine may be needed and what its effects would be. Ritalin is often prescribed for hyperactive children. Though this drug is a stimulant, it works in some unknown way to slow down hyperactive children. It is claimed that it helps them learn better since they can concentrate longer. Critics charge, though, that such medicine is often prescribed to make children behave better rather than to help them learn.

Sports Benefit Handicapped Children

While you will probably be most concerned with your child's classroom education, don't neglect her physical education either, since physical fitness, sports and recreation are as important for the handicapped as for the nonhandicapped. The legislation establishing special education requires that public schools provide handicapped students with physical education and the same recreational opportunities available to nonhandicapped students. Physical activities train and develop muscles, strengthen the heart, provide an overall sense of physical well-being, develop self-esteem, increase mental awareness and present opportunities for socialization with other students, both handicapped and nonhandicapped.

Check to be sure that your child has regularly scheduled physical education classes with nonhandicapped children, if possible. If she is unable to take part in the regular PE classes, what alternatives are available? Does your child receive instruction in such solo sports as swimming and jogging, as well as in exercise programs to stretch and strengthen her muscles? Does your school encourage student participation in the Special Olympics or other sports programs for the handicapped?

There are many groups that provide special recreation and sports opportunities for the handicapped. Talk to the special education coordinator or supervisor at your school to see if sports and recreational activities can be expanded to include such things as wheelchair basketball or square dancing. Also contact the National Handicapped Sports and Recreation Association for more information about groups offering programs. If there are no such programs in your community, you may want to work with other parents in your PTA to provide sports and recreational opportunities outside of school.

Gifted Children Have Special Needs, Too

"I'm often asked why we should worry about gifted children," says Elaine Stienkemeyer, a past president of the National PTA who lives in Hot Springs, Arkansas. " 'Aren't gifted programs a luxury? Can't gifted children take care of themselves?' people ask. My answer is no. These children are the best and the brightest; they are our future scientists, philosophers, artists, and world and business leaders. If they don't accomplish as much as they can, we will shortchange them and our nation, too."

Gifted children may not learn or reach their potential

without extra help from teachers and special programs. Also, gifted children who do not receive help and encouragement often find school boring. This may lead them to do poorly, to become disruptive, to develop emotional problems and even to drop out.

Some critics charge that in educating *all* children, American schools have neglected the best students. Little assistance for the gifted is likely to come from the federal government, although Congress has appropriated small amounts of money for gifted education ever since the passage of the Gifted and Talented Act of 1978, which the National PTA supported. However, when gifted education is available, it is usually a result of state or local initiative rather than federal mandate, and it is paid for by state and local funds. If you want to improve the education for your gifted child, you will most likely have to convince your local school board and superintendent of the need for gifted education.

The Gifted and Talented Act has defined gifted and talented students as those having an outstanding ability to achieve intellectually, creatively, in visual or performing arts or in leadership. This law makes a distinction between the students who do exceptionally well academically and intellectually (the gifted) and the students who have a special ability in a certain area, such as music or sports (the talented). Because this distinction is somewhat arbitrary and many children fit both of these definitions, this book will refer to both groups as "gifted."

Most schools depend on tests, especially on IQ and achievement tests, or a combination of tests and teacher evaluations to determine which students are gifted, but studies have shown that parents are better at predicting whether their children are gifted than are schools. Still, don't jump too quickly to the conclusion that your child is gifted. Some parents put heavy pressure on their children by deciding that they are gifted when in fact they are not.

Generally, gifted children do things earlier, better and in different ways than do other children. Examples of behavior that should alert you to your child's exceptional abilities might be: a one-year-old speaking in long sentences; a two-year-old who asks to take violin lessons; a three-year-old who sits and looks at books for an hour while Grandma reads; a four-year-old who assembles boxes, paper towel tubes, paper and string to make a model of an elevator; a five-year-old who writes books; an eight-year-old who is doing math at the sixth-grade level; a ten-year-old who takes apart your VCR and puts it back together correctly or a fourteen-year-old who is selected as goalie for the state soccer team.

Virginia Ehrlich, a gifted educator, has developed a checklist of traits often found in gifted children. These include early physical and intellectual development, such as crawling, walking, talking, throwing a ball or reading; a large vocabulary; excellent verbal communication skills; an avid interest in books; outstanding memory; ability to learn quickly; creativity; great curiosity; wide range of interests; clear and logical thinking, plus the ability to think in abstract terms and to seek alternative solutions to problems; attention to detail; persistence; self-criticism and high energy. For more information on gifted traits see the Additional Readings section. These national associations and others provide information for parents:

Association for the Gifted (TAG)
(a division of the Council for Exceptional Children)
c/o James Alvino
P.O. Box 115
Sewell, NJ 08080

National Association for Gifted Children (NAGC)
4175 Lovell Road
Circle Pines, MN 55014

You can contact the person who handles gifted and talented programs in your state education department for more information. Also talk with your local PTA president to see if the PTA has programs for the parents of gifted students and if there are other members who are concerned about gifted education.

If you suspect that your child is gifted, you will want to do everything possible to develop her potential. If she is not yet in school, you can read to or with her; provide a wide range of books and magazines, puzzles and toys that she can manipulate and build with; take her to museums and concerts and on nature walks; play word and math games with her; answer her questions and talk with her about everything from superheroes to the Himalayan Mountains. Play make-believe games with her. Mary Renck Jalongo, a professor of early childhood education at Indiana University of Pennsylvania, wrote in *PTA Today,* "Pretending is a way of trying out ideas or solutions to problems," so pretending and fantasizing develop children's creativity and problem-solving skills. Make good use of TV, encouraging your child to watch such shows as "Reading Rainbow," "3-2-1 Contact" and "Square One." Also give extra attention to her physical development—helping her learn to throw a ball and to swim, developing her hand-eye coordination, and working both her small and large muscles.

Being the parent of a gifted child is vastly rewarding, but it can also be difficult and at times intimidating. Most parents of gifted children find that their child's favorite words are "why" and "how." Many gifted children also continually challenge what they hear, see or are told, often challenging their parents even on simple matters by asking questions such as, "Why does it matter if I eat my dessert first as long as I eat all my meat and vegetables afterward?" Questioning and challenging of rules by gifted children, as well as their air of maturity, makes discipline difficult. Guard against falling into the trap of either not enforcing any rules for your gifted child, or of expecting her always to act like a responsible, mature adult rather than like a six-year-old. Of course, when your child finishes discussing how the sophisticated special effects in *Star Wars* were created and then throws a tantrum about taking a bath, you will be reminded that she is six, not twenty-six, and not as advanced emotionally as intellectually.

Most parents of young gifted children make special efforts to find a good preschool. Remember, though, that according to many specialists in early childhood development, a good preschool does not mean one that will teach academic subjects, but rather one that will introduce children to new ideas, experiences and playmates, interest them and help them prepare for school. If your child seems gifted, discuss this with the directors of the preschools you are considering. Be certain that the preschool you choose has lots of toys and materials to be played with, and a trained staff used to working with gifted children.

You may also want to consider whether your child would enjoy music lessons or other special classes before she is old enough for school. Many museums, park districts, community centers and other groups offer classes for young children (with or without their parents) in art, dance, music and dramatics. Many libraries have special story times for preschoolers and early elementary students. Also, in many large cities or suburbs teachers offer the Suzuki method to teach very young children to play the violin or other instruments.

A very good teacher, especially one with a great deal of patience, is necessary for a young child, and parent participation is also vital. For example, parents are expected to attend both private and group Suzuki lessons, and to practice with their children at home. While the idea of involving your child in music at an early age is appealing, getting a preschooler or kindergartner to practice the violin can be a tremendous struggle.

Be careful not to schedule a young child for too many activities. She learns most through play, so don't consider time at the park or working with toys at home as wasted. Gifted children often make good use of unstructured time to explore things that interest them.

Gifted-Child Programs

As your gifted child approaches the age of four, you may begin thinking of the possibility of early admission to school. In order for them to enroll in kindergarten, many states now require that all children be five at the start of or early in the school year, though some allow early admission for those children who are more mature than others. Before thinking about early admission for your child, talk to her preschool teacher about whether she is ready to do well in school. If your child has never attended preschool, it might be wise to enroll her in one, rather than to send her directly to kindergarten. Even if your child is a preschool veteran, consider carefully whether she is as mature emotionally, socially and physically as she is intellectually. Most educators agree that, no matter how gifted, it is a mistake to enroll children in school early if they will be unable to adjust to school or to make friends.

If you decide to ask or petition for early admission, your child will probably have to take readiness tests to assess her emotional, social, physical and intellectual development. If she is granted permission to enter early, she will probably be the youngest member of the class, which may mean that she will be slower than other children in adjusting to school. Discuss your child's age and abilities with the kindergarten teacher, who may be able to provide special assistance to help your child get into the school routine. If she is not mature enough socially or emotionally, she may find school difficult and confusing, so think carefully before starting her in school early.

If you decide not to seek early admission, or if the school does not allow it, see that the year at preschool or home is filled with the kinds of activities that stimulate and interest your child, plus lots of time for vigorous play out of doors. Then, when she starts school the next year, discuss with the teacher your child's abilities and what you have observed about her learning style. Kindergarten teachers depend heavily on repetition, teaching the same idea or skill again and again until all the children have mastered it, but if your child is a quick learner, she may grasp what is being taught after the second time she hears it. See if the teacher can plan ways to keep your child interested so she doesn't tune out when, for example, the teacher discusses the seasons for the twentieth time.

Also alert the teacher if your child already knows how to read. While many gifted children make everyone around them aware of just how much they know, others are so quiet that they might go for months before the teacher realizes they have mastered reading. Discuss how you and the teacher can work together to provide extra help for your gifted child. Ask about special books, material, assignments or programs, but be careful not to act like a pushy, demanding parent.

Many schools don't begin special programs for gifted children until the third or fourth grade, with more attention being paid to gifted children as they move up in school. Virginia Ehrlich has estimated that schools meet the special needs of only about 35 percent of gifted children. In the early grades your child may be placed according to ability in certain reading and math groups within her regular classes, a placement that will allow her to move ahead at her own speed. Some schools keep the more academically talented students together for most or all of the day. Many schools also have enrichment programs that provide gifted students with extra help and encouragement from trained teachers. Most of these programs are called "pullouts," since students are pulled out of their regular classrooms and sent to a separate room for special work. Many schools do not provide as much enrichment or assistance as gifted students need.

At least by the time your child starts school, you will want to obtain a copy of your district's gifted and talented plan (if it has one), and you may want to talk to the gifted and talented coordinator or supervisor, or to the principal, if there is no other staff member in charge of gifted education. Among the key things to learn is how children are selected for gifted programs. Is selection based on tests? On teacher nomination? On some sign of creativity or talent, or on a combination of several of these? Determine if tests are used only to exclude students. You may want to challenge a system under which an IQ or other test eliminates your child from a gifted program when all other signs point to her exceptional ability and talent.

Learn what programs are available for gifted students and also how the teachers for these programs are selected and trained. Are the school board, superintendent and principals committed to gifted education? This you can ascertain by talking to your local PTA president, to a PTA member concerned about gifted education or to a member of a local association of parents of gifted children, if there is one in your community.

Once your child is settled in school and doing well, your next big decision may be whether to request or to allow her to skip a grade. A few schools, such as magnet schools for the gifted, have stopped basing grade level on age, thus allowing students to move through school at their own speed, but the closest most schools can come to freeing gifted children to move ahead at their own speed is to let them skip a grade. Some school districts are quick to suggest that gifted students skip grades, while others are very hesitant.

Among the dangers of moving children ahead are that they may not be mature enough to handle new, older classmates and that the greater academic demands may put too heavy a strain on them. Consider very carefully before deciding to allow your child to skip a grade. Some parents, who either skipped a grade themselves or who know someone else who was unhappy with the results, adamantly refuse even to consider moving their children ahead. Others think that their children are mature enough to handle such a move and see skipping a grade as a way for their children to get ahead rapidly and be less bored.

In *Parents' Guide to Raising a Gifted Child,* James Alvino recommends that students meet several criteria before being allowed to skip a grade. These criteria include high achievement and IQ, either good grades or signs that boredom is causing them to be underachievers, the ability to work independently, a greater capacity than most children of their age to make decisions and express feelings, and a preference for older friends. Only if your child meets all these criteria, and only if she wants to move ahead, should you consider advancing her.

Since some children who have been doing very well suddenly suffer socially or academically after skipping a grade, the decision to advance your child may be a difficult one—even with all these criteria in place. If you or your child has any doubts about skipping a grade, probably the best advice is not to unless the situation in her current grade is intolerable.

Problems Facing Gifted Students

Like all children, the gifted have individual strengths and needs, so one program will not serve all gifted children. Whatever talents or abilities yours possesses, she will benefit most if a special program or plan can be developed to accommodate her individual needs and ways of learning. For this reason, some gifted advocates believe that schools should prepare special plans similar to IEPs (individualized education programs) for gifted children. Few, however, do so. What you will usually find is that your child will be provided with a few enrichment classes for about an hour once or twice a week. In addition, classroom teachers may assign extra work, reading or projects that go beyond what is offered in the regular curriculum. Your child may have the opportunity to prepare special research papers, read extra or more difficult books, and do independent experiments to augment what she has learned in class and to keep her interested and challenged. Some teachers have also found that having gifted children work one-on-one with slower students in their class benefits both groups.

In spite of efforts to assist gifted students at your child's school, her ability to reach her potential may well depend on her own resourcefulness and your assistance outside of school. You'll want to encourage her to learn as much as possible in school and to discourage her from coasting through on her ability. But as your child moves beyond the early elementary years, don't be surprised if you depend heavily on books and outside activities to offer her stimulation and enrichment. Such activities can round out your child's education and provide interest and incentive for her to learn on her own.

While it may be difficult to find help for all gifted children, James Alvino points out that three groups of gifted students in particular are likely to be overlooked: the gifted handicapped, gifted minorities and gifted girls. The term "gifted handicapped" may seem like a contradiction until you think about a few examples—a physically handicapped but intellectually gifted child, a retarded but musically talented child or an outstanding runner who is hearing-impaired. In such cases, there is a strong tendency for parents and schools to concentrate on the handicap and overlook the gifts. If you believe your handicapped child is also gifted, be sure to bring this up at the IEP planning meeting, and insist that special programs be implemented to develop her gifts.

Minority children, especially those from low-income, culturally disadvantaged or non-English-speaking homes, are underrepresented in gifted programs. Often schools need to use nontraditional ways to evaluate their talents and abilities.

While girls make up more than half of the gifted students in the early grades, as the years pass the percentage of gifted girls decreases. Most likely, this change occurs in part because many teachers, like many parents, treat boys differently from girls. For example, many teachers reward boys for being curious and asking questions while encouraging girls to be quiet and cooperative. They tend to credit boys' success to their intellectual abilities, attributing girls' achievements instead to hard work. This, in turn, helps convince boys that they are bright and capable, and girls, that they aren't. Also, peer pressure—particularly pressure to be popular and never to be "different"—leads many gifted girls to hide their abilities. Even today, in most schools girls are admired more for their beauty, clothes and boyfriends than for their achievements. Often girls are not encouraged to take "hard" subjects like physics and calculus. They are channeled instead into languages and the humanities.

The pressure to mask their ability, to achieve less than they are capable of, affects boys as well as girls, because many children (and even some adults) make fun of gifted students. For this reason, you will want to help your child feel good about her talents but not flaunt them. Don't encourage your child to select only gifted children for her friends, either. She needs to share things besides academics, so help her select friends with different interests and abilities. Even if your child lives and breathes math or music, encourage her to broaden her interests, and be especially sure she has enough time to play, to exercise her muscles as well as her brain. Work with her to set realistic goals. Don't expect that she will be gifted at everything she does. Even if she has a high IQ and does outstanding work in most of her classes, there may be some subjects in which she doesn't excel. So don't make your child think she is a failure if she doesn't always get an A or is not the best student in all her classes.

Parents of gifted children often forget to praise their children's successes. If your child brings home a report card with four A's and one B, congratulate her for the A's rather than focusing on the B. Many gifted children tend to be perfectionists and are never satisfied with their work or with themselves, so take every opportunity to build your child's self-esteem. Children should know that they are loved for themselves, not for their high IQ or for their ability to play the piano. Finally, as James Alvino wrote in *PTA Today,* "Let them act their age. A gifted child is still a child. Don't push your child to be a miniature adult. Expect the very young scholar or violin virtuoso to be egocentric, sometimes selfish and capable of throwing tantrums—just like other youngsters."

PTAs in Action

Many PTAs have programs to help children with special needs, and some PTAs are set up just to help special education students. These PTAs, often called SEPTAs (special education PTAs), may serve all special education children in a community or in a school for the handicapped. Other PTAs have individual sections for parents of gifted children and parents of handicapped children. The PTA can be an excellent ally for them in their efforts to get the best education for their children. These are just some PTAs that help special students:

- The Sorenson Special Education Combined SEPTA in Kirkland, Washington, is attached to a school for disabled, gifted and regular students. Because so many different groups are served by this one school, the PTA works to create a feeling of unity among them. Each year it sponsors an open house/ice cream social and a school carnival so all parents and students can get to know each other.

• The Katherine Butterworth PTA in Moline, Illinois, provides an "Art Connection" program for special education and gifted children as well as for others in their school. The PTA arranges for graduate students from the University of Iowa to visit the school, where they offer students hands-on experience in music, dance, art and creative writing.

• The College View SEPTA in La Crescenta, California, which serves a school for severely handicapped children aged four to twenty-two, sponsors a Sunday "Handicamp" every four to six weeks. It opens the school to students, parents, siblings and friends of the disabled children, who all gather for an afternoon of family fun. The handicapped and non-handicapped have the opportunity to play together and get to know each other.

• Helping students make the most of their future is one of the goals of the West Babylon SEPTA in West Babylon, New York. Each year it holds a college night so that students in special education and their parents can learn about colleges with programs for special education students.

• The Ysleta Learning Center SEPTA in El Paso, Texas, provides monthly workshops on topics of interest to the parents of handicapped children. It also distributes a newsletter and a booklet listing helpful community agencies. One of its special projects is a "Need/Find" program, which provides services such as free help with the preparation of legal guardianship papers, to assure that handicapped children will be cared for after their parents' deaths.

• The Edward S. Snow PTA in Dearborn, Michigan, created an "All Kids Are Special" program to educate parents about learning disabilities. Included were parent workshops on topics such as effective discipline, hyperactive children and sibling rivalry.

• The James E. Allen Melville SEPTA in Copiague, New York, holds an annual orientation for bus drivers during which school staff and SEPTA leaders discuss medical, behavioral and safety issues relating to the transportation of special children.

• The Islip SEPTA in Islip, New York, presented a pregnancy information program for teenagers that stressed the importance of prenatal care in preventing birth defects.

• The Paramus Special Education PTA in Paramus, New Jersey, sponsors a four-week summer program, Camp Horizon, at which students can swim, take trips and have fun. It also provides art classes, a physical education program and an after-school activity center.

• The Sixth District PTA of Santa Clara County in San Jose, California, has a unique program to help blind students. For more than thirty years the PTA has done free transcribing of textbooks and other school materials into Braille, and it has made the transcriptions available to any student in America or abroad for the cost of duplicating. It takes three or four pages of Braille text to transcribe a page of print, so a 753-page textbook might end up with, say, 2,667 Braille pages. Since a skilled PTA volunteer may work for fifteen to twenty minutes to put a printed page into Braille, it takes 160 PTA volunteers many hours each week to get the transcriptions done. To serve the blind in their community, the volunteers also transcribe such diverse materials as games, greeting cards and wills. Some members also tape-record literature.

• Unless you have a child who is handicapped or know someone well who is, you probably have no idea what it means to be handicapped. To help the nonhandicapped understand a little about the life of the handicapped, the Decatur City Council PTA in Decatur, Alabama, sponsors a handicapped awareness week in cooperation with its local public schools, the local chapter of the Association for Retarded

Citizens and the Tennessee Valley Rehabilitation Center. Students are shown videotapes focusing on the problems that handicapped children face. Tours of the city's special education facilities are given, and at the end of the week PTA members help with the Morgan County Special Olympics.

- The Washington Village PTA in Washington Village, Vermont, conducted a meeting on learning disabilities and the importance of appropriate educational programs so that parents whose children did not have such learning handicaps would understand the needs of learning disabled children and their families.

CHAPTER

8

Keeping Kids Healthy

YOU'VE READ AND heard a great deal about young people's problems with alcohol, drugs, sex and pregnancy, but you may well think that these are threats to other people's children, not to yours. "My son wouldn't use cocaine, and anyway, we don't live in the kind of community where drugs are available," you tell yourself. "And his dad has told him about the facts of life, so we don't have anything to worry about with sex," you add. But are you sure? The soaring teen pregnancy rate, fears generated by AIDS and recognition of the widespread use of drugs such as alcohol and crack are forcing many parents to take a hard new look at the need to guard their children's health. Are you doing as much as you should to protect your child?

"Parents are learning that prevention is the key to keeping children and teens healthy," says Glenna Gundell, a former chairman of the National PTA's Health and Welfare Commission. But to be successful, prevention requires that parents and schools work together—with parents teaching their children about drugs, alcohol, cigarettes, sex and AIDS (as well as how to develop a healthful lifestyle), and with schools reinforcing those messages.

"One parental lecture on the evils of drug abuse or an easy admonition such as 'Just Say No' isn't enough to prevent children from experimenting with drugs and sex, which can ruin their lives and even kill them," continues Gundell. Instead parents need to set good examples for their children, encourage them to get good nutrition and plenty of exercise, and talk to them early and often about potential dangers. Schools need to present the facts about healthful and unhealthful behaviors, guide children to make wise decisions and establish patterns that will promote their good health.

Schools have always been involved in children's health. Early American schools taught hand washing and other basic elements of personal hygiene. With the advent of universal public education in the late nineteenth century, schools became concerned with the prevention of contagious diseases. Children were checked at school for everything from TB to lice, and those found suffering from an infectious disease were promptly sent home until they recovered. Schools have provided screening for noncontagious health problems (vision and hearing impairments, scoliosis, etc.) and PTAs have been active in encouraging and assisting with such screenings. Throughout the years schools have also taken a lead in seeing that children are immunized against various diseases.

Over the last decades schools have turned much of their attention away from contagious diseases and toward the idea of maintaining good health in already healthy youngsters; thus, in today's schools, you will hear health educators talk about "wellness" and prevention.

Most parents want their children to learn about health in school. The National PTA supports comprehensive health education in the nation's schools, believing that a unified, carefully planned program of health instruction is a high priority and urging that such programs be developed and funded in all schools. It also suggests that family life education; nutrition; dental, mental and environmental health;

physical fitness and accident prevention; plus such specific subjects as alcohol and drug abuse, smoking, sexuality, sexual and other forms of child abuse, AIDS and other sexually transmitted diseases (STDs) be covered in health programs.

Unfortunately, the quality of health education varies from state to state and school to school. Many states require that children receive some type of health education. Check the regulations in your state and school district to learn, for example, if a certain number of hours of health education are required for high school graduation. Also ask about the health curriculum. Although most states have some regulations about health education, many decisions are left to local school officials. This has both pluses and minuses, because health education can change rapidly if new concerns develop, or it can be cut just as rapidly if a local school runs short of funds or if priorities change.

Most health education in elementary schools is taught by the regular classroom teacher. In some high schools, health education classes are taught by teachers well trained and certified in this field, but in other schools, health education is assigned to any teacher who happens to have a free period. See if the subject is taught by properly trained health educators in your high school, and if elementary teachers are prepared to be effective health educators also.

According to a recent assessment by the American School Health Association, the average student in kindergarten through sixth grade is required to take 47.5 hours of health education a year, the average seventh and eighth grader a little over 40 hours and the average high school student only about 21 hours. But a major study found that it took at least 50 hours of health education a year to teach students effectively about health, and to change their attitudes and practices. Check the number of hours required in the different grades in your child's school.

AIDS Education

AIDS is an epidemic that is as frightening as it is deadly because there is no cure in sight and no vaccine to prevent it. "The National PTA believes that teens and children should be educated about AIDS both at home and at school, since only by parents and schools working together can young people be fully protected," says Laura Abraham, head of the National PTA's AIDS project. Entitled "AIDS Education at Home and School: PTAs Respond to the Need," this program was developed with funding from the Centers for Disease Control. Polls have shown that the American public agrees that AIDS education is necessary in the schools and that teens badly want more AIDS instruction. "Because of the gravity of the AIDS threat and the need for more information about it, the National PTA has called for AIDS education to be instituted in all schools in America, and is helping local PTAs educate parents about AIDS so that they can in turn educate their children," explains Abraham.

Such education is necessary, because anyone of any race or ethnic background—man or woman, heterosexual or homosexual, old or young—can get AIDS. Although so far teens have accounted for less than one percent of AIDS cases, health experts say that they are especially at risk because of experimentation with sex and drugs. Also, over 20 percent of AIDS victims are in their twenties. Given the long incubation period for AIDS, it is believed that many were infected as teens.

Former U.S. Surgeon General C. Everett Koop has recommended that education about AIDS begin in elementary school. Check to see if your school offers AIDS education. If not, encourage the school board and superintendent to institute such a program immediately, and ask your local PTA president to plan a meeting about AIDS for parents. If your school already teaches about AIDS, you will want to evaluate the strength of the AIDS curriculum.

Here are some questions you can ask your principal or local PTA president to assess the effectiveness of your school's AIDS curriculum: Are educators given special training to teach the curriculum? Are they comfortable teaching about AIDS? Is instruction given in clear, direct language? Does it provide information to both preteens and teens? Is education appropriate for the age groups taught? Does it stress the fact that *anyone* who practices high-risk behavior such as having multiple sex partners or sharing drug needles can get AIDS? Does it provide information about how to avoid getting AIDS? Were parents, teachers, health and curriculum specialists, and students involved in developing the curriculum? Is it reviewed and updated often? Are time and materials provided adequate? What student activities does it suggest? Does it teach decision-making and problem-solving skills aimed at helping students avoid risk-taking behaviors? Does the curriculum encourage students to communicate openly and often with their parents?

Beware of a simplistic approach to AIDS. It isn't enough for an AIDS curriculum merely to tell young people not to have sex or to use drugs. William L. Yarber, a professor at Indiana University and recognized authority on AIDS education, noted in *PTA Today* that a sound AIDS curriculum should stress the personal behaviors that put one at risk for contracting AIDS and the behaviors that help avoid it. "Most current curricula do list abstinence as the most effective preventive strategy," he writes. "Despite moral proscriptions, many young people have chosen to be sexually active. Therefore it seems reasonable that the school provide complete preventive information. . . . The 'Just Say No' approach used in drug education is inappropriate for AIDS education, since equating sex with drug abuse may teach adolescents to be unduly afraid of sex. Schools should acknowledge the positive aspects of sexuality by teaching young people to value and respect sex and to use sex wisely and responsibly."

What Parents Need to Know About AIDS

Even if your school teaches about AIDS, you must still talk to your child about the ways to prevent contracting it in order to be sure that he truly gets the message. Know the facts about AIDS yourself. Before reading further, take the "How Much Do You Know About AIDS?" quiz below. Unless you know the answers to all the questions, you have a lot of studying to do. To begin, you will need to know that AIDS (Acquired Immunodeficiency Syndrome) is caused by a virus that attacks a person's immune system, making the

HOW MUCH DO YOU KNOW ABOUT AIDS?

True or False:

1. The main ways that the AIDS virus is spread are through sexual contact and the sharing of IV drug needles with a person who carries the AIDS virus.
2. A few people have contracted AIDS from touching the tears or saliva of a person with AIDS.
3. You can't get AIDS from shaking hands, hugging, eating in restaurants, sharing dishes, toilets, telephones, swimming pools and office machinery, or by being the friend of a person with AIDS.
4. Colds, flu and measles are passed through sneezing, sharing glasses and being around an infected person. A child can catch AIDS in these ways, so children with AIDS should be kept far away from healthy children and from schools.
5. You can tell which people have the AIDS virus, since they always look sick.
6. When used the correct way, condoms can lower the risk of getting AIDS.
7. Less than half of teens have sexual intercourse before age twenty.
8. Teens and preteens have little chance of getting AIDS, so they and their parents need not worry about it.
9. Teens can avoid getting AIDS by not having sex or using IV drugs.
10. Young people already know all they need to about AIDS.

❦ ❦ ❦

body unable to fight off infection and disease. Most people contract AIDS through sexual contact or through the sharing of intravenous (IV) drug needles or syringes with someone who carries the AIDS virus. Infants can be infected if their mothers have the AIDS virus during pregnancy, childbirth or breast-feeding. Before 1985 blood for transfusions was not tested for AIDS, so some people—including most of the school-age children with AIDS—were infected in this way.

How is AIDS *not* spread? You can't get AIDS from everyday social contact with someone who has AIDS. This means that you can't get it from touching or hugging someone;

Answers

1. True. **2.** False. Although small amounts of the virus have been found in tears and saliva, there have been no reported cases of the AIDS virus being passed in this way. **3.** True. **4.** False. AIDS is passed in other ways. The U.S. Surgeon General, the Centers for Disease Control and the National PTA believe that most children with AIDS pose no threat to other children, and they belong in school. **5.** False. Though an infected person may have no outward signs of the virus, he can still spread it to others. **6.** True. However, condoms must be used for all sexual contact, and care must be taken that they don't leak or break. You can further lower the risk of infection by using condoms with a spermicide containing the chemical nonoxynol-9. **7.** False. A 1986 report of the Alan Guttmacher Institute found that 70 percent of girls and 80 percent of boys have had sexual intercourse by the time they reach their twentieth birthday. **8.** False. Because many teens and preteens experiment with sex and drugs, they are at risk for contracting AIDS. Therefore, they and their parents must know how to avoid getting this deadly virus. **9.** True. But because so many teens are already sexually active, you may want to stress that using condoms lowers the risk of getting AIDS. **10.** False. Many young people know dangerously little about AIDS. That is why the Surgeon General has recommended that AIDS education begin in elementary school and why the National PTA has called for all parents and schools to teach about AIDS.

using a drinking fountain, swimming pool or public restroom; eating in a restaurant; or sharing a sandwich, soda, chewed pencil, item of clothing or typewriter. While colds, flu, measles and chicken pox are easily spread through sneezing, coughing, using the same straws or just being around someone who is sick, you can't "catch" AIDS like this. In fact, long-term studies of family members living with adults or children with AIDS show that no one in the home has become infected through routine, nonsexual contact. While small amounts of the AIDS virus have been found in tears and saliva, there have been no reported cases of AIDS being transmitted in these ways. You can't get AIDS from donating blood, either, since sterile equipment is always used.

Many parents have a hard time discussing AIDS with their children, but talking with them about this deadly threat is vitally important. As much as you might wish to, you can't control your youngster's behavior, so the best way to protect him is to educate him. Don't let discomfort or nervousness prevent you from discussing AIDS. Don't wait for your child to ask questions. Instead, learn accurate information about AIDS and discuss it in understandable ways. Find out what your child thinks he knows about AIDS, and correct any misinformation. Finally, reassure him that, while AIDS is dangerous, he can avoid it.

Preschoolers may have heard the word "AIDS," but few are ready for a complicated discussion of it. Instead, this is a good age to begin to talk about sex. Most important, you want to let your child know that you are open to all his questions. Children between the ages of five and eight should be told that AIDS is a serious health problem, that it is caused by a virus and that very few children get AIDS. Preteens from nine to twelve are ready for more information. Since the AIDS virus is most commonly spread by sexual contact and drug use, it is important that your preteen get the correct information about sex and drugs. Warn him of the dangers of casual sex and IV drug use, and be sure he understands your beliefs and values relating to both sex and drugs.

Because so many teens are sexually active today, they should be told that the more sex partners they have, the greater the risk of becoming infected. In fact, a single sexual contact with an infected person can be enough to give a person the AIDS virus. Therefore, the best protection from AIDS for teens is to avoid sex. If they are sexually active, both teens and adults should practice the safest sex possible. This means not exchanging body fluids, including semen, blood or vaginal secretions. When used the correct way, latex condoms can lower the chances of men and women getting AIDS. Condoms should be used during all types of sexual contact. A foam, cream or gel spermicide or a condom containing nonoxynol-9 may help lower the risk even more. Be sure that your teen also recognizes the hazards of using IV drugs and of sharing drug needles or syringes.

Most Children with AIDS Belong in School

None of the reported cases of AIDS in the United States has been transmitted in a school, day-care center or foster-care home. "The Surgeon General and the Centers for Disease Control have stated that in most cases children with AIDS or infected with the AIDS virus belong in school, and the National PTA agrees," states Abraham. "Also, teachers or other school staff who have AIDS or are infected with the AIDS virus do not pose a health risk to your children."

When a child has AIDS, his doctor, parents, public health officials and school personnel should decide whether he is able to attend school. This decision should be made on an individual basis, as would be the case for any health problem. If a child in your school has AIDS or if a family member, relative or friend gets AIDS, you should offer support, compassion and understanding. Continue friendly, nonsexual

IF A CHILD IN YOUR SCHOOL HAS AIDS

1. Don't panic!
2. Learn the facts about AIDS. Your school may send home AIDS education materials for you to read. It may schedule a meeting to discuss AIDS and allow parents to ask questions. If you receive no information, ask your PTA president or principal to call a meeting. Other good sources of information include your local health department or the 24-hour toll-free AIDS Hotline operated by the U.S. Public Health Service: (800) 342-AIDS.
3. Once you are comfortable with your knowledge of AIDS, talk with your child. If your child is young, reassure him that his chances of getting AIDS are very, very small. A teen or preteen should be warned of the dangers of casual sex and IV drug use. In addition, let your child know that it is safe to go to school and to play with children with AIDS.
4. Learn what AIDS education your school is offering to students and staff. The National PTA believes that all schools should provide AIDS education, but don't depend on the school to tell your child all he needs to know about AIDS.
5. Most schools have already adopted routine procedures for handling blood and body fluids from any child or staff member who has an accident or becomes injured at school. Check to be sure that your school has such a plan in place.
6. Offer support, compassion and understanding to the child and his family. Remember—the child and his family pose no threats to your child. To repeat, none of the reported cases of AIDS in the United States has been transmitted in a school, day-care or foster-care setting. And in most cases, the Surgeon General, the Centers for Disease Control and the National PTA believe that children with AIDS belong in school.

contact. Medical and health experts assure parents that it is safe for children to play, sit near and be friendly with a child with AIDS. The National PTA has gone on record as opposing boycotts, marches and other protests against children infected with AIDS attending schools because it recognizes that the fight is against a health problem, not against children or adults with AIDS.

Evaluating a Sex Education Program

The threat of AIDS has given renewed impetus to sex education in schools. For a number of years polls have shown that sex education has been supported by a large majority of parents. For example, the 1987 Gallup/Phi Delta Kappa survey showed that 82 percent of parents with children in public schools thought that high schools should teach sex education, while 60 percent thought that sex education should be taught in grades 4 through 8 as well. In discussing the AIDS epidemic, former U.S. Surgeon General Koop said that there is now "no doubt" that sex education should be taught in the schools. Yet timidity on the part of school boards and administrators, or the influence of a few vocal opponents has prevented many schools from offering effective sex education courses.

While some schools teach AIDS education separately from sex education, it makes more sense to offer a comprehensive health education curriculum. Yet, according to a recent publication by Irving Dickman and Sol Gordon entitled *Schools and Sex Education,* only two states have mandated comprehensive sex education courses for their schools. In a number of other states, sex education is encouraged, and many school districts have instituted courses and curriculum, often called "family life education," which contain information about sex and other topics. Still, it is estimated that fewer than 15 percent of students get a really good sex education.

Check what sex education is offered in your school. You might ask: Is it a part of a comprehensive health education program? Is it taught by a specially trained teacher who is both knowledgeable and comfortable with the subject? How many hours are allotted to sex education? (According to Dickman and Gordon, over the four years students are in high school, they may receive only five to ten hours of sex education in health or physical education classes.) Does it teach only anatomy and reproduction, or does it cover a wide range of topics related to sexuality, including feelings and values, respect for others, pregnancy and contraception, masturbation, advantages of delaying sexual activity until older, sexually transmitted diseases (including AIDS), heterosexuality and homosexuality, ways to avoid date rape, problem-solving and decision-making skills, and how sexuality contributes to a happy and healthy life?

If your school offers no sex education, ask your PTA president to call a meeting so that parents can discuss the need for it. If you are concerned about the effectiveness of the program, discuss it with the principal or the health education teacher and ask for a PTA or school meeting to consider how the program can be strengthened. Find out how parents can participate in planning and implementing the program as well as in coordinating what is being taught at school with what is being taught at home. Numerous studies have found that when parents participate in planning and implementing sex education and other forms of health education, there are fewer controversies and the programs are stronger. Also, as Dickman and Gordon state, "Experience shows that parents' involvement nearly always increases parent-child communication about sexuality and sexual behavior."

Birds and Bees

While sex education in schools is important, parents should provide the primary sex education for their children. Although most parents recognize that it is their responsibility to explain to their children about sex and sexuality, two out of three parents have great difficulty talking with their children about these subjects. In fact, it is estimated that fewer than 20 percent of parents have ever had a significant conversation with their children about sex. Have you talked with your child about sex? What have you said?

"Talking with your children about sex gives you an opportunity to teach them to feel good about being a man or woman," says 1989 National PTA presidential nominee Ann Lynch. "Studies have shown that children who talk with their parents about sexual feelings and decisions are more likely to delay sexual activity. But the main reason you should talk with your children about sex is that sex involves family values, feelings and communication. No one is better suited to educate your children about such matters than you."

Parents often wonder at what age they should talk to their children about sex. You should talk to your child at all ages. You can't just give him one facts-of-life lecture and think your job is done. Year after year you must talk to him and share your beliefs and values. Start early. Your child's sexual feelings and attitudes begin to develop from birth. He takes his first important step toward a healthy sexuality by observing family interactions, so you can provide a good model by showing affection toward family members and by holding and cuddling your newborn baby. Also nurture your child's self-esteem, since young people who feel valued and who value themselves are less vulnerable to pressures to engage in sex.

As your child becomes a toddler and then preschooler, you should talk to him about his body and respond to his questions. Teach him the correct terms for the genitals, try to answer his questions matter-of-factly and honestly, and provide information in words he can understand. A good rule of thumb is to give your child a little more information than he may want, but not to overload him with details. For example, you may want to tell a four-year-old that before he was born he spent nine months in his mother's uterus, but don't try to explain exactly how he got there unless he asks.

Remember the example of the child who, when he asked his mother where he came from and received a long reproduction lecture, responded, "But what I wanted to know was, did I come from Cincinnati or Cleveland?"

By the time your child begins school, he is ready for more detailed information. Children aged five to nine are interested in the mechanics of reproduction and the meaning of words. Most experts agree that if your child hasn't asked any questions about sex by age five or six, you should take the initiative. Chances are he is getting information, often wrong information, from other children or is afraid to approach you about the subject.

Children aged nine to twelve need both more information and reassurance. If you talk about the anxieties you suffered as you entered puberty, you can reassure your child that what he is going through is normal. Be sure that you explain the changes that will come before the onset of puberty, and remember that children today enter puberty at an earlier age than they did in the past. For this reason, many sex educators recommend that parents tell their children no later than age ten about menstruation and "wet dreams" as well as about sexual feelings and desires. Many parents find it helpful to give their children a book or brochure about puberty. See the suggestions in the Additional Readings, and ask your local librarian, the health teacher at your school or your local chapter of the Planned Parenthood Federation of America for suggestions.

Many parents avoid talking to their preteens and teens about sex because they believe that their children are already well informed about the subject. But, in reality, young people are very ill informed. Other parents postpone talks because they think it is too early to discuss sexual feelings and desires with, say, an eleven-year-old. Parents who believe that they can wait until their children are older are wrong. Statistics show that about 4 percent of twelve-year-olds are already sexually active, and the percentage goes up rapidly from that age on. For teens, sexual activity too often leads to pregnancy. With more than 1.1 million teenage pregnancies each year, America leads the industrial nations of the world in the rate of teen pregnancy. If present trends continue, every fourteen-year-old girl in America today will have a 40-percent chance of becoming pregnant at least once before she is twenty.

According to a National PTA brochure entitled *How to Talk to Your Preteen and Teen about Sex,* you should cover the following topics: reproductive systems of both sexes; sexual intercourse; fertility and birth control; masturbation; forms of sexual behavior besides intercourse, such as necking and petting; sexual feelings and desires; responsible sexual behavior, including never taking advantage of or coercing another person to have sex; possible negative physical and emotional consequences of sexual intercourse, such as teen pregnancy, sexually transmitted diseases (including AIDS), the blow to self-esteem that can come from the end of a sexual relationship, and ways to avoid sexual abuse and date rape. While covering the potential problems caused by sexuality, you should also convey to your child the message that sexuality is a beautiful and important part of his life.

Many teens don't want to start sexual activity but feel that they must if they are to be like all the other kids. Therefore, encourage your child not to become sexually active by telling him that not everyone is having sex, and that he may be better prepared for a sexual relationship when he is older. Discuss with your daughter possible responses to such lines as "You would if you really loved me." One response might be "If you really loved me, you wouldn't ask me to do something I'm not ready to do." And discuss with your son his responsibility not to pressure someone to have sex. Parents should discuss pregnancy and birth control with both sons and daughters. Such discussions don't give them permission to have sex but rather remind them of the possible conse-

TEACH YOUR CHILD DECISION MAKING

Being able to make good decisions is critical to maintaining health and safety, whether by avoiding AIDS, not using alcohol and other drugs, or by delaying sexual activity. Here are some ways to help your child learn to make good decisions:

- Give your child opportunities to practice making decisions, such as selecting his own clothes, dividing up household chores or choosing the site for a family outing.
- Show your child how to weigh his options, gather necessary information, consider alternatives and predict potential outcomes of his decisions.
- Help your child understand that decisions have consequences both for himself and others, and teach him to take responsibility for his decisions and actions.
- Show your child that when he avoids dealing with a problem and fails to make a decision, this can be as bad as his making the wrong decision.
- Accept your child's decisions as long as they aren't dangerous. Support his ability to make decisions by understanding that many of them are based on personal tastes and needs, and may not be the same ones you would have made.
- Keep in mind that a child who exercises some control over his life has higher self-esteem. The ability to make decisions helps prepare him to become a responsible, happy adult.

quences of sexual activity and of their responsibility to prevent unwanted pregnancies.

Children today are exposed to a continuing hard sell about sex through TV, movies, magazines and rock music. If you are having a difficult time initiating a conversation with your child about sex, use a TV show, a magazine ad or a visit from a friend with a new baby as a springboard for your talk. Watch for opportune moments and encourage communication and openness by planning time alone with your child each week. However, don't insist that your child talk about sex. Offer information and try to balance TV's messages about sexuality by commenting on the shows you watch together. Make books available to read together or for your child to read on his own, but don't force the issue, and don't lecture. Remember that while you want to guide your child to make the best decisions about sex, you can't make these decisions for him.

Date Rape

In date or acquaintance rape, the rapist is unlikely to use a weapon, relying instead on limited amounts of force and threats, or on verbal coercion. Teenage girls are at special risk for date rape since they may be less careful about the situations they get into, and because many lack the self-confidence to say no loudly and effectively enough to discourage this form of assault. Also, some teenage males glorify date rape, viewing it as a macho form of seduction, with the perpetrators claiming that the young girl really wants to have sex and just needs a little forcing to go through with it.

Tell your daughter about date rape and make sure she realizes an attack may come from someone she knows and leasts expects, such as the boy next door or the captain of the football team. Tell her always to be careful to avoid places where she will be alone with someone she doesn't know well or doesn't trust. Even if she knows her date well, she should watch for situations that make her uncomfortable. Date rapists are less likely to attack girls who seem self-confident and assertive. Therefore, if someone tries to pressure your daughter to go somewhere she doesn't want to, or to force her to engage in sexual activity against her wishes, she should say loudly and clearly, "Stop! Don't do that! I don't like it." If possible, she should then immediately leave and seek help. Screaming may also deter a date rapist. If nothing works and your daughter is assaulted by a date, encourage her to report the attack, since date rapists often prey upon young women in a community. Talk to your son about date rape, too. Be sure he realizes that such behavior is illegal, harmful and wrong.

School-based Health Clinics

Are school-based or school-linked health clinics a means to help students deal with sexuality? Do they provide much needed health care for teens, or do they intrude on roles that should be reserved for parents? Will they lower teen pregnancy rates or encourage promiscuity? These are some of the questions you will hear whenever school-based health clinics are mentioned.

By 1987 there were more than one hundred health clinics based in or linked with public schools across the nation, with an additional hundred in the planning stages. These clinics provide primary health care for teens, including physical exams, first aid, immunization, education to prevent drug and alcohol abuse, counseling about sexuality, family planning information, pregnancy tests and treatment for sexually transmitted diseases. Most also provide mental health services and counseling, health education and referrals to outside doctors, programs and agencies.

Sharon Lovick, director of The Support Center for School-based Clinics, believes school-based health clinics are needed because many teenagers do not receive adequate health care despite their high rate of health problems and injuries. Research done by the center found that fewer than 25 percent of the total services of these clinics relate to reproduction, and that 79 percent of clinics do not dispense contraceptives. Other research has found that clinics in areas such as Baltimore, Maryland; Jackson, Mississippi; and St. Paul, Minnesota, have dramatically lowered teen pregnancy rates. Counseling provided by the clinics also seems to have led students to delay sexual activity.

Most school-based health clinics require written parental consent in order for children to receive medical care. Most clinics also have an advisory board with representatives from the school, parents, health experts, students and religious organizations. While some parents have protested against clinics, most parents in schools with clinics support them, and in a number of cases clinics have been created at the instigation of parents and parent groups. The National PTA recommends that schools considering the formation of such clinics develop an advisory committee to determine their feasibility and desirability, and to monitor their operations once established. If the trend of the last few years continues and parents and communities grow increasingly concerned about teenage sexual activity and AIDS prevention, more school-based health clinics will probably be established. If your high school lacks a school-based health clinic, and if the students' health needs are not being met, discuss with other parents and your PTA whether a clinic would be helpful or whether there is another way to get health services for students who need them.

Facts About Alcohol and Other Drugs

Drug abuse among young people escalated rapidly in the 1970s. Though use of most drugs has leveled off or even declined slightly in recent years, it is still very high. For example, a University of Michigan survey released in early 1988 found that 57 percent of high school seniors had used an illicit drug (besides alcohol) at least once in their lives, 42 percent had used an illicit drug during the past year, more than one third had tried a drug other than marijuana, more than 10 percent had tried cocaine at least once (with 4.3 percent being current users of cocaine), and 5.6 percent had tried crack, a cheap and highly addictive form of cocaine. While all of these figures were down somewhat from earlier years, the percentage of seniors having tried alcohol rose, with estimates from other studies ranging up to well over 90 percent.

"Most parents worry about drug abuse, but often they think that *their* children aren't in much danger," says Jeanne Koepsell, a health specialist with the National PTA. Many

HOW MUCH DO YOU KNOW ABOUT DRUGS?

1. Which country has the highest rate of drug abuse?
   a. Italy
   b. France
   c. the United States
   d. Mexico
2. The drug used most often by American high school seniors is:
   a. marijuana
   b. alcohol
   c. cocaine
   d. cigarettes
3. Alcohol is not as dangerous as drugs.
   a. true
   b. false
4. What is the leading cause of death among teenagers?
   a. drunk driving
   b. infectious diseases
   c. drowning
   d. AIDS
5. Drug abuse by teens is escalating rapidly.
   a. true
   b. false
6. You can wait until your child is a teenager to talk to him about alcohol and other drugs.
   a. true
   b. false

❦ ❦ ❦

parents also ignore, wink at or accept their children's most frequently used drug—alcohol. "I know they drink beer, but at least they aren't taking drugs," these parents say. This ignores the fact that alcohol is a drug, and that alcohol use for young people is both dangerous and illegal. Parents and young people must realize that alcohol can ruin children's

7. What is the most frequent cause of premature death among adults in the world?
   a. AIDS
   b. wars
   c. famine
   d. cigarettes
8. Because of all the education about the dangers of smoking, few young people are smoking today.
   a. true
   b. false

Answers

1. c. The drug rate in the United States is two to ten times higher than that of any other Western democracy. **2. b.** While nearly two thirds of high school seniors have tried other drugs, as many as nine out of ten may have used alcohol. **3. false.** Alcohol *is* a drug, and for underage young people alcohol is an illegal drug. **4. a.** More teens die of alcohol-related car crashes than any other cause. **5. false.** In the last few years the number of teens using drugs has declined slightly except for the number of those using alcohol, which has continued to rise. **6. false.** Children as young as nine and ten years old say that they have felt pressure to use drugs, 8 percent of sixth graders smoke marijuana and there are possibly as many as 3 million alcoholics under the age of eighteen in this country. Therefore, you need to talk to your child about drugs and alcohol when he is very young. **7. d.** It is estimated that worldwide in 1985, between 2 and 2.5 million smokers died of heart disease, lung cancer, emphysema and other diseases caused by smoking. Cigarettes are deadly. **8. false.** Approximately 30 percent of high school seniors have smoked cigarettes in the last month. Many are daily smokers.

health. Heavy partying often plays havoc with schoolwork and family relationships. Alcohol combined with driving results in the number one cause of death among teens—drunk driving. "For these reasons you need to be concerned if your children use alcohol or other drugs, and you should be sure that your school teaches about alcohol and drug abuse as a part of its comprehensive health education curriculum. Most of all, though, you will want to talk to your children often about drugs and alcohol and about why they should not use them," Koepsell adds.

The average American youth first tries alcohol or other drugs between the ages of eleven and fourteen, so you need to start educating your child early. The National School Boards Association (NSBA) recently urged schools to develop a strategy of prevention that includes a drug education curriculum beginning in kindergarten and continuing through high school. The program should explain the effects and the dangers of alcohol and drugs as well as help students deal with peer pressure.

Check the drug and alcohol abuse prevention curriculum in your school. If your school doesn't teach about drug and alcohol abuse prevention, ask your PTA president to call a meeting to discuss prevention education, or talk to your principal.

When checking on your school's drug and alcohol curriculum, also check the discipline policy related to drug use and sale at school. According to the National School Boards Association, schools need a clear, written policy prohibiting on-site student drug or alcohol use, backed up with strong enforcement. They should also assure that drugs are not sold at school either by students or outsiders. Schools should confront students suspected of using drugs and help them get treatment. This three-part program of education, keeping drugs and alcohol out of schools, and encouraging treatment will be more effective, NSBA contends, than any plan to test

A CHECKLIST FOR EVALUATING DRUG EDUCATION IN YOUR SCHOOL

1. Our school offers drug and alcohol abuse prevention education.
   ____yes ____no
2. It is offered in grades ______________________________.
3. It includes:
   ____drug facts ____alcohol facts ____tobacco facts
   ____information on improving self-esteem
   ____coping skills ____refusal skills
   ____ways to deal with peer pressure
   ____other: ______________________________.
4. It also includes information about drug use in this community.
   ____yes ____no
5. It is taught as a part of these classes:
   ____health ____social studies ____science ____P.E.
   ____other classes: ______________________________.
6. Teachers are trained in drug and alcohol education.
   ____yes ____no
7. The school uses the following drug and alcohol education curricula: ________
   ______________________________.
8. The following films, books and pamphlets are used in classes: ________
   ____
   ______________________________.
9. Parents participate in the school's drug and alcohol education program.
   ____yes ____no
   If yes, how?______________________________
   ____
   ____
10. Does the school allow smoking on campus?
    ____yes ____no
    If yes, ____by students ____by faculty
    ____only in designated areas ____elsewhere ____________.

students for drugs or to search students and their lockers. Does your school have a drug and alcohol prevention plan? If not, encourage it to implement one immediately.

Teach About Drugs and Alcohol at Home, Too

As with other health problems, what your child learns about drugs and alcohol in school is important, but what he learns at home is even more important. Discuss drugs and alcohol with your child from the time that he is young. Explain the rules you expect him to follow about alcohol and drugs, and the reasons behind these rules. Let him know that rules such as never using drugs or riding with someone who has been drinking must not be violated. Be sure he understands the consequences of his breaking these rules, and enforce the rules you make.

You can better protect your child by first understanding why teens and even preteens are motivated to drink and use drugs. Young people usually say that they do these things to have fun, because everyone else does it, to look cool and grown up, and because it is exciting. Often teens feel pressured to use drugs or to drink in order to be one of the gang. For this reason, you need to help your child learn to handle peer pressure. This means finding friends who share his interests and values, and having enough self-esteem to stand up to pressure. Sometimes a quick, one-line response is helpful. Work out with your child responses such as "No thanks—I've got other things to do tonight" or "No, my folks could smell booze a mile away." Tell your child to give his response and then leave—he shouldn't stay where others are using drugs or alcohol because these activities are illegal and because after a while peer pressure might get too much for him to withstand.

In addition to talking to your child about alcohol and drugs, you need to set a good example. Since actions speak louder than words, take a hard look at your own drinking and drug use. Be especially careful not to give your child the idea that any drugs, whether alcohol, tranquilizers or cigarettes, can solve problems. Discuss with him your use or nonuse of alcohol and drugs. Be candid about your efforts to change dangerous habits such as smoking and drinking too much. Encourage your youngster to practice healthful activities such as getting plenty of exercise, eating the right foods and coping with stress.

Jeanne Koepsell encourages parents to give their teens and younger children solid information about how alcohol and other drugs affect the body. "They don't need unrealistic scare stories such as telling them that if they use a certain drug they will die, since they may know kids who have used that drug with no apparent problem," she says. "Instead, your teens need an unemotional and factual discussion of the effects of drugs and alcohol on the body, and what it feels like to be high or to have a hangover." Also make sure that your child knows the law—that drug use and underage use of alcohol are illegal and might lead to his arrest. Since so much teen alcohol and drug use is built around parties, insist that your teen not attend parties where alcohol and drugs are used or where parents are absent. Continues Koepsell, "Be absolutely certain that *your* home is never used for drug or drinking parties, and that a responsible adult is present at any party in your home or that your children attend."

Parents in some communities have joined together to alert police to parties where drugs and alcohol are being used, to force the cancellation of "keg parties," to encourage liquor stores to abide by laws banning the sale of alcohol to underage customers and to set up pledge programs, in which parents promise to remain home for all parties at their house and to forbid the use of drugs or alcohol.

Don't ignore these signs of drug or alcohol abuse: preoccupation with partying, a decrease in extracurricular activities,

KEEP TEEN PARTIES ALCOHOL- AND DRUG-FREE

Since young people often use drugs and alcohol at parties, work with other parents in your community to keep the parties alcohol- and drug-free.

If your teen is the host:

- Set the ground rules in advance. Specify, for example, the number of guests permitted, the off-limits areas of the house, the presence of lighting, and the ban on all drugs and alcohol.
- Insist that adults be visible at the party itself, not just occupied elsewhere in the home. Walk through the party occasionally, mingling briefly with the guests to see that things are under control and that your child doesn't need help.
- Help your teen plan a fun party, perhaps a theme party, without drugs or alcohol. Have him consider an activity such as renting a video camera to film his guests performing favorite rock songs.
- Obey curfew and all other laws. Insist that he keep the noise down so that neighbors won't be annoyed or tempted to call the police.
- Consider ruling that no one who leaves the party can return, since teens sometimes leave a party to drink or use drugs and then try to come back.
- Most important, *serve only nonalcoholic beverages, and allow no drugs!* Be prepared to send away anyone who disobeys these rules and to call the parents of any guests causing trouble.

If your teen is a guest:

- Know the host's name, address and phone number.
- Call the host's parents in advance to confirm that they will be home. You may feel uncomfortable doing this, but you may be able to ease the awkwardness by asking if you can send refreshments or help in another way.
- Be sure to verify plans for any overnight stay.
- If possible, be at home while your child is at the party. If you can't be home, give your child a phone number where you can be reached, and arrange for him to call another trusted adult if he can't contact you.
- Agree with your child that he will call home if he gets into trouble and that you will not blame him for his friends' behavior.

sudden problems at school, neglect of personal appearance and hygiene, violent behavior, hostility, secretiveness about friends and a marked change in sleeping or eating habits. Often parents will have a general feeling that something is wrong and will see small changes in their child's patterns and habits. Don't ignore these changes, but don't jump to conclusions, either, and accuse your child of using drugs when he may just be going through a normal teenage phase.

Many counselors suggest that parents confront their children if they suspect drug use. You might say something like "I'm worried that you may be using alcohol and drugs. Can we work on this together before it becomes a bigger problem?" If you are not able to help your child solve his problems, call your doctor, the school counselor, a local mental health center or a group such as Al-Anon or Alcoholics Anonymous and ask for help or a referral to someone who can help. Don't shut your eyes but rather seek help immediately.

Suicide Prevention

There is probably nothing more devastating to parents than to have a child commit suicide. Although in the last few years the number of teen suicides has plateaued after having increased substantially in previous decades, more attention has been paid to this problem in part because of the occurrence of suicide clusters, in which four, five or more young people in a community take their own lives in rapid succession. Even where there has been no such rash of suicides, parents need to be aware that suicide remains the second leading cause of death among the nation's fifteen- to nineteen-year-olds, with an estimated 1,500 to 2,000 teenage suicides each year.

There is no single cause of suicide or type of youth that is likely to commit suicide. Those who attempt or commit suicide come from all socioeconomic groups. Some teens have been using drugs or alcohol. Some have shown signs of violent or self-destructive actions, while others have shown no outward signs of problems. Some have been under stress because of school, sports, dating or other factors, while other students who are under equal pressure never consider taking their own life.

Many schools have added suicide prevention to their curricula. While some experts fear that spotlighting teen suicide in classes or through TV shows may in fact encourage students to commit suicide, many others believe that sensitively and carefully taught classes can help dissuade students from suicide. Also important are suicide prevention hotlines, counseling and mental health programs for troubled teens. Teachers, parents and fellow students alike should be alert to the warning signs of teen suicide, taking seriously any threats or comments about suicide.

Teaching a Healthful Lifestyle

In addition to suicide prevention, many school health programs teach stress reduction, nutrition, the dangers of smoking (often taught along with drug and alcohol abuse prevention), physical fitness, personal safety and ways to develop a healthful lifestyle. In a well-planned curriculum, the teaching of health extends beyond traditional health classes into science and physical education classes, and sometimes into social studies and English classes as well.

As you evaluate the quality of health education your school provides, pay close attention to physical education. Many American youth are not physically fit. Studies, reported by the President's Council on Physical Fitness and Sports, have found that 40 percent of all children aged five to eight show some risk factors of heart disease such as high blood pressure, high cholesterol or physical inactivity. Childhood obesity is also increasing as children spend more time watching TV, playing video games and eating junk food than running around outside and playing. Daily physical education and sports at

WARNING SIGNS OF TEEN SUICIDE

According to the American Academy of Pediatrics, the following are warning signs of possible teen suicide:

- Preoccupation with death.
- Changes in eating or sleeping habits.
- Unexplained or unusually rebellious or disruptive behavior.
- Depression and withdrawal.
- Running away.
- Persistent boredom or difficulty concentrating.
- Drug and alcohol abuse.
- Failing grades.
- Unusual neglect of appearance.
- Radical personality change.
- Psychosomatic complaints.
- Giving away prized possessions.
- Expressing suicidal thoughts, even in a joking manner.

If either your child or his friends show several of these signs or the most dangerous of them, such as expressing suicidal thoughts, giving away possessions or preoccupation with death, get help immediately. Contact your doctor, school counselor, local mental health association, suicide hotline or crisis center.

school, and vigorous physical activity at home are ways to keep youngsters fit and healthy.

Only about 36 percent of students in grades five through twelve receive daily physical education. Find out how much P.E. students take in your child's school. Many experts recommend at least one period a day of vigorous activity, not just play. Find out, too, what is taught in P.E. Is all the time spent playing such competitive sports as softball, volleyball and basketball, or are students taught sports and activities that they can do throughout their entire life, such as swimming, aerobic dancing, jogging and tennis? Do students work on developing agility, strength and endurance? Do they exercise vigorously enough to strengthen their cardiovascular system? How much of each P.E. period is spent in challenging physical activity and how much is spent in administration and in waiting to take turns? Are students tested? Are those in need of special help with flexibility, strength or weight control identified and helped?

At home set a good example for your child by showing him that regular physical exercise is important to you. Best of all, exercise and play games with your child. Set time aside three or four times a week to run, jump, play, swim or do other vigorous activities with him. Consider putting a weekly chart on the refrigerator and giving all family members a "smiley face" when they exercise. Set a limit on the amount of time that your child can watch TV, and get him outside to play as much as possible. If you have a yard, set up things that he can climb, play and swing on, or regularly take him to a playground. Be sure that he learns to swim. Swimming is the best possible exercise, and knowing how may someday save his life.

In order to stay healthy, children and teens need to learn about nutrition, accident prevention and environmental dangers. Keeping children healthy has always been one of parents' chief responsibilities, but today that responsibility is shared with the schools. It is only when parents and schools work together, coordinating and reinforcing the same message, that you can be certain your child will have the best chance of developing a healthful lifestyle for all his tomorrows.

PTAs in Action

Almost all PTAs work to improve the health of the children and teens in their community. Some hold health fairs or help with vision and hearing screening. Others develop programs to teach good health practices to students in their community, and most hold meetings for parents to discuss such health-related topics as AIDS, drug and alcohol abuse, nutrition, teen suicide, stress and physical fitness. Many local and council PTAs use a packet of material entitled "Parenting—The Underdeveloped Skill," produced by the National PTA and the March of Dimes, to conduct meetings on how parents can communicate better with their children and build young people's self-esteem.

As part of its nationwide program "AIDS Education at Home and School—PTAs Respond to the Need," the National PTA called for all PTAs to hold meetings to educate parents about this dreaded health problem and to rally support for AIDS education in their school. Of the hundreds of PTAs that responded in the first year alone, here are some examples of the actions they took:

- PTA leaders at James Madison High School in Vienna, Virginia, successfully urged the school board to implement a comprehensive curriculum about AIDS and presented a panel discussion on "AIDS and the Adolescent." When a child with AIDS was enrolled in the county school system, a representative of the James Madison PTA was asked to serve on the ad hoc committee set up to establish an AIDS policy for all schools.

• When the Alachua County school board in Florida mandated that schools provide AIDS education, the Gainesville High PTSA was asked to coordinate the school's AIDS program. The PTA conducted a pretest to find out what students knew about AIDS, arranged for a lecture on AIDS, brought in the Gainesville Area Improvisational Teen Theatre to demonstrate role-playing for students, helped to develop a role-playing packet for teachers to use and conducted a posttest, which found that students had learned a great deal about AIDS and its prevention.

• Leaders of the Shawnee Mission East PTA in Shawnee Mission, Kansas, helped write a curriculum for ninth and tenth graders on human sexuality that included AIDS education. They organized an AIDS assembly for eleventh and twelfth graders, and an AIDS symposium for parents of students at their high school, two middle schools, nine elementary schools and for the general public.

• The Wilton High School PTSA in Wilton, Connecticut, was part of an AIDS education coalition that developed a program for students and parents. The PTA sponsored an AIDS conference and helped plan for AIDS Education Day at Wilton High School.

• The Beverly Hills High School PTA in Beverly Hills, California, conducted a parent meeting and helped plan a full-day program for seniors, plus a teacher education program.

• When the Goodland Elementary School PTA in Racine, Wisconsin, polled its members to see what topics parents and teachers wanted the PTA to cover, the vote was nearly unanimous for a program on AIDS. Therefore, the PTA scheduled a meeting with local health experts and distributed material to parents.

• When a Carter County PTA leader in Van Buren, Missouri, first suggested an AIDS education meeting, AIDS seemed very far away from that community. But, soon the PTA board became convinced that a meeting was necessary. Materials were distributed at this and other PTA meetings, as well as throughout the town.

• The Redmond Junior High PTSA in Redmond, Washington, was part of a planning group that developed a special presentation for students and established an AIDS curriculum.

• The Lincoln Elementary School PTA in Salinas, California, which serves a school that is heavily non-English-speaking, received a grant from the Hispanic Policy Institute to present a program on AIDS. It was attended by 95 percent of the parents.

• Another PTA found itself on the firing line when a child in its school tested positive for AIDS. Rumors swept through the rural Maryland community of Caroline County and panic was about to set in when the superintendent of schools, the principal of Denton Elementary School, the Denton Elementary PTA, the Caroline County PTA Council, the teachers, the school board and the local press got together to defuse the situation. The principal asked the PTA to call a special meeting to provide parents and school staff with expert information and to allow them to ask questions. Over three hundred people turned out for a three-hour meeting, which immediately lowered tensions. Following the meeting, the school developed and publicized safety procedures for dealing with any accident or injury at school. Of the 685 students in the school, only 2 were removed by their parents.

For more than ninety years the National PTA has worked to end the use of drugs, alcohol and tobacco products. To help in this effort, it designated the first full week in March as Drug and Alcohol Awareness Week, and thousands of PTAs have conducted programs to combat drug and alcohol abuse either during that week or at other times throughout the year. The National PTA has distributed more than 1.5 million brochures on alcohol and other types of drug abuse, plus more than twenty thousand planning kits to help local

PTAs and councils develop programs. It is currently launching a multiyear, multimillion-dollar project funded by the GTE Foundation, a part of the GTE Corporation, to prevent drug and alcohol use by nine- to fourteen-year-old students. Also, with funding from the National Highway Traffic Safety Administration, the PTA has provided high school PTAs with information about programs to help prevent teen alcohol use and eliminate drunk driving. Many PTAs sponsor Project Graduation, which aims at assuring safe, alcohol-free proms and graduation parties. The National PTA has also given monetary grants to a number of PTA councils to help them develop drug and alcohol abuse prevention projects.

Here are some examples of PTAs that have fought drug and alcohol use:

• The Norwalk/La Mirada PTA Council in California created a "Mobile Drug Education Unit" that travels to schools in the area to teach third and fourth graders not to use drugs.

• The Burlington PTA Council in Burlington, Iowa, developed a sixth-grade drug education program, which includes four meetings for students. The program has been so successful that school counselors have asked to take it over.

• The Clayton County PTA Council in Georgia set up a Red Ribbon Commission to encourage students to stay drug-free. It has produced a series of Gold Medal posters displaying prominent sports stars and their messages about not using drugs and alcohol.

• The Milwaukee PTA Council in Wisconsin selected one middle school as the target of a special program to try to stamp out drug use among at-risk students.

• Drug and alcohol abuse prevention are two of the topics covered in a series of educational workshops called "Bridging the Gap" that the Crabapple Middle School PTA in Roswell, Georgia, ran for parents, students and teachers. Other topics included parent-child communication on sexuality and self-esteem.

• When a number of young people were killed in alcohol-related auto accidents within an eighteen-month period, the Livingston Parent-Teacher Council in Livingston, New Jersey, developed a "Safe Home program." Parents pledged not to allow parties in their home unless they are present and to ban the use of alcohol and drugs. The New Jersey PTA endorsed the plan, as did National PTA convention delegates.

• When the Vernon Township PTA, also in New Jersey, became concerned about drug paraphernalia, it brought a resolution outlawing them to its state PTA. In time the PTA succeeded in getting the bill passed by the New Jersey State Legislature.

Here are some additional highlights of PTA activities related to children's health:

• The Clayton County Council of PTAs in Georgia has developed award-winning programs on teen sexuality, teen pregnancy, the safety of latchkey children, child abuse and drug abuse. It established "Growing Up and Understanding It" workshops for youngsters aged nine to fifteen, a teen pregnancy-prevention program called "Let's Talk" and a workshop series to help parents understand and deal with their teenagers.

• The North Charleston Elementary School PTA in South Carolina held a program on stress management for elementary school children and sent information home to parents.

• The Germantown Elementary School PTA in Germantown, Tennessee, conducted a program entitled "Let's Learn It Together," aimed at helping parents learn to talk and listen to their children.

• The Millbrook High School PTA in Raleigh, North Carolina, created a "Lifestyle '87" program after parents expressed disbelief upon learning of alcohol use at teen parties in their community. The program brought teens and parents together for an evening to discuss problems young people face, and to help parents and children learn to communicate better. Topics covered were teen stress, family communication and self-esteem.

• Stress was also one of the concerns of the Echo Mountain PTA in Phoenix, Arizona, when it arranged to open an on-site counseling center, with specialists available one day a week, to aid students, staff and parents. The Echo Mountain PTA also held a school workshop on stress management for students and school staff. In addition, it started a "Dealing with Divorce" program for students.

• The Nixa PTA in rural Missouri created a five-week series of seminars, reaching almost 250 parents, on topics such as adolescent sexuality, self-esteem, single parenting and the media's effect on children. The PTA also set up a parenting library at the school.

• Following an outbreak of teen suicides in Plano, Texas, the Richardson PTA Council suggested a two-evening program on suicide prevention for teens, parents and teachers. As part of the program a video was made and shown on a local cable TV station, and a copy was placed in the school library for students and teachers.

• Jefferson County, Colorado, suffered a similar rash of teen suicides, which led the PTA and other community groups to organize a county-wide suicide prevention program. A Suicide Prevention Task Force for Jeffco Youth was formed, and crisis teams were set up within schools to create a suicide prevention plan as well as a response plan in the event of a suicide. The Jefferson County PTSA participated in these activities and organized many of its own, such as creating a Parent Information Network (which distributes packets of information to all PTAs) and sponsoring the Jeffco's Pride Allstar Revue, a performing troupe of students from seven Jefferson County high schools that stages a musical review to promote self-esteem and community pride.

• The Lakewood High School PTSA in Jefferson County, Colorado, worked with the school counseling staff to assemble, print and distribute a booklet entitled *Teen and Parent Help Line*.

• The Basset PTA Council in La Puente, California, has also developed a suicide prevention program and operates a suicide prevention hotline.

• The Wilmore Davis PTA in Wheat Ridge, Colorado, approached health from a different angle when it started the Wilmore Davis Health Club in the gym of its elementary school and offered thirty-minute aerobics classes three times a week for teachers, students, parents and community members.

• The White Oak Elementary School PTA in White Oak, Pennsylvania, sponsored a "Feeling Good" program to supplement regular physical education classes. Conducted in cooperation with the local YMCA, the program offered forty-five-minute activity sessions every other week. Students from kindergarten through fourth grade learned about the benefits of vigorous physical exercise and good nutrition, developed their cardiovascular systems and had a lot of fun exercising together.

• The Bellevue PTA in Bellevue, Kentucky, held an all-day health fair. More than forty organizations displayed information and services to the students, parents and community members who attended.

• The Greenwood School PTA in Des Moines, Iowa, helped put on a safety fair as part of the school's week-long safety program. Puppets were used to teach students about seat belts, street safety, drunk driving and other dangers.

• The Frederick Douglass PTA in Seaford, Delaware, became concerned about fire safety in its town, so it applied for and received a grant from the National Community Volunteer Fire Prevention Program to set up its own fire safety plan. As part of this plan, the PTA encouraged the school to establish a "Learn Not to Burn" workshop for elementary school teachers. It also hosted a fire safety program for its community and set up displays throughout the year at local shopping malls telling about fire safety and the need for smoke detectors.

• Fire safety is also a major concern of the Indiana State PTA and of PTA members in Mishawaka, Indiana, who along with the Mishawaka Fire Department created a "Survive Alive House"—a safety training center that teaches children about fire safety through the use of simulated fires. Groups of schoolchildren go through the Survive Alive House, plan escape routes and practice what they would do in various fire situations. Other PTAs across the nation, including the Chicago Region PTA, are working to set up similar projects in their communities.

CHAPTER

9

Making Your Voice Heard

BECAUSE RICK AND Mitzi Alley of Cincinnati, Ohio, like rock music, it was natural that when they bought a new album a few years ago, they would select the latest one by a performer whose songs they had heard on the radio. However, soon after they had settled down to enjoy the music with their children, both parents dashed to turn off the record player so that their children wouldn't hear one of the song's sexually graphic lyrics. As the Alleys thought about this afterward, they became convinced that albums should have warning labels to let purchasers know if they contain material inappropriate for children. For the Alleys it was never a question of censoring such albums but of providing consumer information—of knowing what you or your child is buying before you get home.

The Alleys wanted to express their opinion on the need for warning labels and raised their concern at the next PTA meeting, where many parents agreed with them. The Delshire Elementary School PTA sent a resolution calling for record labeling to the National PTA Convention. It was adopted, and the National PTA called upon the recording industry to put a warning label on material that included sexually explicit or violent lyrics or that glorified drug or other substance abuse. Subsequently, the National PTA testified on the issue before a U.S. Senate committee. After more than a year of negotiations with the Recording Industry Association of America, the National PTA and the Parents' Music Resource Center (a group based in Washington, D.C.) won a major victory. Twenty of the nation's top music producers agreed either to identify future releases containing lyrics about explicit sex, violence or substance abuse with the label "Explicit Lyrics—Parental Advisory" or to display the complete printed lyrics on the record jackets. With help from the PTA, the Alleys and other parents had made the recording industry listen.

Phyllis Sheps and other PTA leaders from the West Orange Council of PTAs in West Orange, New Jersey, believed that the drinking age should be raised to twenty-one in order to lessen the vandalism problems in their community, and because they were aware of the high number of eighteen- to twenty-year-olds killed in alcohol-related automobile accidents. So PTA leaders took the issue to the New Jersey State PTA and to the National PTA. This led to the formation of the Coalition for 21 in New Jersey, which spread the cry across the country. Today in all fifty states and the District of Columbia, twenty-one is the mandatory drinking age thanks in large measure to parents who recognized the power of making their voices heard.

Former National PTA president Manya Ungar first got involved with the PTA when she learned her son's school was so overcrowded that kindergartners were going to have to attend school in three shifts—some going very early in the morning and others late into the afternoon. The area around the school had no crossing guards, no traffic signals and no sidewalks. Yet, the school district couldn't win community support for a bond issue to build new classrooms, the state wouldn't erect a stoplight unless citizens could prove that it was needed and the town council wouldn't put in sidewalks. Consequently, a small band of PTA parents had to take on three levels of government. This they did with gusto, organizing parent patrols to count cars, mounting letter-writing campaigns, providing testimony to the county and state governments and engaging in other forms of community action. And they won—the school received voter approval to build the needed classrooms, the state put up a stoplight and the community put in sidewalks—all because a group of parents made their voices heard.

National PTA presidential nominee Ann Lynch and parents from the Fremont Junior High PTA in Las Vegas, Nevada, were concerned because their children had to eat lunch outside, with the sun beating down upon them mercilessly in the warm months. The school district said it didn't have the money for an indoor lunchroom and offered no other help, so the PTA leaders went to the Las Vegas PTA Council, which studied the problem and called for a bond issue. PTA members worked to educate community leaders and citizens about the issue, and the bond referendum was passed. It provided money for a multipurpose room where students could eat in comfort. Because PTA members knew how to make their voices heard, all Las Vegas schools now have such a facility.

Making your voice heard doesn't always guarantee a victory, however. Van Mueller, a PTA leader from St. Paul, Minnesota, and other PTA members in that state believed strongly that public tax money should be used only for public schools. They filed suit against a law that provided a tax deduction for the expenses parents paid if their children attended private or public schools and were charged a fee to participate in extracurricular activities such as athletics or debate. With support from the Minnesota State PTA and the National PTA, the case, *Mueller* v. *Allen,* made its way through the courts until it was finally heard by the U.S. Supreme

Court, which ruled that this deduction was constitutional. Once more a group of citizens had found a way to express their concerns and opinions, in this case, to the highest court in the nation.

These are all examples of how parents have made their voices heard by working together, through their local, council, state and National PTAs. Other PTA parents have fought to get lunch served in their school, to pass state legislation mandating child safety seats for autos and to pass federal laws requiring the inspection of schools for asbestos. "Working together, especially working through their PTA, parents can accomplish much, much more than they could if they worked alone," says Pat Henry, a PTA leader from Lawton, Oklahoma. "Parents will find that they are never alone when they unite with others—parents and nonparents alike—to improve the life, health, education and safety of children."

On a Local Level

To make your voice heard in your school, you must be thoroughly acquainted with that school. Learn about the school structure; financing and budget; rules; state and federal regulations; curriculum; facilities; discipline policies; support services; teachers; school and student needs; and efforts to improve the education it offers. To help parents gather facts about their local school, the National PTA has issued *Looking in on Your School*. Parents can use this workbook as the basis of a PTA or other group project to evaluate their school's strengths and weaknesses and to suggest improvements. The checklist included in the workbook gives you important questions to ask about your school's goals and objectives, administration, teachers, students, curriculum, support services, library/media or learning center, school plant and financing, parents and community. You can learn a great deal about what your school needs to do to assure educational excellence for all the children it serves.

KEYS TO AN EFFECTIVE SCHOOL

- A strong principal who is an instructional leader as well as an administrator, and who involves staff, students, parents and community in the school.
- Clearly stated goals and rules that are understood and accepted by students, staff and parents.
- Expectations that all students will achieve their potential and the means to help them do so.
- Emphasis on academics, especially reading, math and communications skills.
- A carefully planned testing and evaluation program to pinpoint student strengths and weaknesses.
- Committed, caring and skilled teachers who actively involve students in learning.
- A pleasant, safe and orderly but not rigid environment for students and staff.
- Encouragement for students, staff and parents to participate in setting directions for the school.
- An administration and staff that are open to change and to parents' participation in their children's education.
- Parents committed to learning and deeply involved in their children's education.

However you gather facts about your school, you will find the job easier if you work with other parents and community members, since a group can almost always accomplish more than an individual or couple. Once you have clearly identified goals, begin with your group to plan how to achieve them. Get as much input as possible from other parents, school staff, students and community members, then develop concrete suggestions for improvement with achievable time lines. Be sure to enlist the support of those who have the authority to make necessary changes—the school board, superintendent, principal, teachers or local government authorities. Investigate the procedures for speaking at board of education meetings and for raising issues. Most boards have a period for public comment or discussion. Use this time as a way of generating interest in your group's ideas.

Actions that you might propose for your school include:

- Establishing a program to monitor school board meetings, with parents and PTA leaders attending all meetings and presenting statements or comments as appropriate.
- Calling for a long-range planning committee.
- Suggesting an update of the school's goals and objectives and its discipline code.
- Abolishing corporal punishment.
- Starting a school-age child-care program.
- Creating a community-school budget committee.
- Appointing a community-school selection committee for books and other school materials.
- Correcting safety hazards, for example, by implementing a more rigorous program to train bus drivers, by removing "friable," or flaking, asbestos from the school ceiling, or by building a pedestrian overpass to allow students to cross a busy highway.

Investigate the rights and responsibilities of parents at your school. How well are parents carrying out their responsibilities, such as assuring that their children attend school? Is the school guaranteeing parents' rights to participate in their children's education? Is a campaign to make parents aware of their vital role in their children's education needed, or should parents impress upon the school their desire to help monitor school activities and participate in decision making?

Many districts have established policies that encourage parent participation in both their own child's education and in helping to govern the school. If your district has no such policy or the policy is weak, encourage your PTA to work to strengthen it. Help the PTA ensure that parent involvement is truly welcomed at your school.

A PARENT'S RIGHTS AND RESPONSIBILITIES

The National PTA believes that the primary responsibility for the education of children lies with the family. Parent involvement begins before the child's birth and should continue until the child reaches adulthood. That involvement takes many forms, including parents' sharing of responsibility in decisions about the child's education. In 1986 the National PTA board of directors passed a parent involvement statement, which reads, in part:

A parent, as a role model and initial teacher, has a *responsibility* to:

- Safeguard and nurture the physical, mental, social and spiritual education of the child.
- Instill respect for self, for others and for learning.
- Provide opportunities for interaction with other children and adults.
- Lay the foundation for responsible citizenship.
- Provide a home environment that encourages and sets an example for the child's commitment to learning.
- Know, help and interact with the child's teachers and administrators.
- Participate in the selection of responsible school board members.

A parent has a *right* to have:

- Clear, correct and complete information about the school and his individual child's progress.
- Confidentiality of information about her individual child.
- Clear understanding of the processes to gain access to the appropriate school officials, to participate in decisions that are made and to appeal matters pertaining to his individual child.

What if no one listens when you make your wishes and views known? If you have talked to the classroom teacher and the principal about specific problems and nothing has been done to improve the situation, you can take your concerns to the superintendent and the school board. If the concern is bigger than a problem with one teacher or one school, you will probably need to go directly to the superintendent or school board. It is important always to work your way up the leadership ladder when discussing problems or making suggestions, but it is equally important to reach the person who can do whatever you think should be done. In many cases it is only at the central administration office that you will find someone who can make the changes you want.

However you decide to make your voice heard, you will get a better reception if you come as a member of a group of parents and if you have carefully done your homework. Thus, for example, if you think that budget priorities should be reevaluated and more money spent on the academic curriculum, your presentation will be more effective if you can cite facts, figures, the testimony of experts and specific areas where funds could be shifted. Your case will also be more likely to succeed if you and your supporters present your views in a calm, professional manner. Don't attack the superintendent as incompetent and then expect an enthusiastic response to your suggestions for changes. Don't call the school board members do-nothing bums. Instead try to involve school officials in your plans, and if this is not possible, at least recognize that they are probably trying to do their best.

Public opinion is one of your most important allies. Imagine, for example, you are campaigning to have the school buses equipped with mirrors that allow the driver better visibility in front of the bus in order to see children hidden by the hood. First research bus safety and the number of children hit by their own school buses both in your state and nationally. Then present your case at a PTA meeting and line up supporters to attend a school board or community meeting. If school board rules allow, ask for your concern to be placed on the agenda, or see if a school board member will raise the topic. If you can't get it on the official agenda, plan to speak during the time allowed for citizen comment and arrange for supporters to back you up. Contact the editor and the education writer at your local newspaper, and at your local TV and radio stations; explain the problem and the suggested solution; ask for news coverage and editorial support. Organize a letter-writing campaign to the school board and the newspaper. Consider a petition drive so that your group can demonstrate wide community support when time for a school board or community meeting rolls around. Distribute flyers and use other means to alert community members and parents to the concern. Publicize the upcoming meeting, since a good turnout of people on your side will go a long way toward convincing officials to look into the matter.

If none of these maneuvers persuades the school board or local government officials to help solve the problem, you will most likely have to turn to public pressure or to the courts. You may also have to work to see that more responsive school board members are selected or elected. Don't be discouraged if your efforts fail to produce immediate results. Joan Ball and other New York State PTA leaders worked for more than fourteen years before finally convincing the New York State Legislature to outlaw corporal punishment in New York schools. It has taken even longer to awaken the public, Congress, the Environmental Protection Agency and local school officials to the need for asbestos removal from schools. Be persistent. Make yourself an expert on whatever subject you choose to pursue.

In Your State Capital and Washington

You may be hesitant, as are many parents, about trying to influence legislation, policies and regulations on the state or national level, but working together with other parents, you *can* make your wishes known. Your local, council, state and National PTA will help you, since they possess expertise in legislation and other government activities. In addition, the PTA can marshal thousands of other parents to support you. When an association with more than 6 million members speaks, everyone listens.

"If you see a problem that needs to be addressed by your state government or that you want to bring to the attention of the federal government in Washington, begin by talking to your local PTA president," advises 1989 National PTA presidential nominee Ann Lynch. Many local PTAs have a legislative committee chairman who can be an extremely valuable resource. "If you can't get the help you need through your local PTA, see if your PTA is a part of a PTA council —a group of local PTAs that agree to band together for mutual support. If you strike out here, too, contact your state PTA office and ask for the name of your state legislative chairman or another PTA member who can help." For example, if you are worried about a health issue such as AIDS education in your school, ask for the state health chairman's name as well as the legislative chairman.

"Most state PTAs are actively involved in supporting legislation that will improve children's lives, health, safety, education and welfare, so you will probably find that a state PTA leader is already working on your issue," continues Lynch. Most states have several PTA leaders, including a legislative chairman, who spend a lot of time in the state capital monitoring legislation and making the PTA's and parents' views known on issues affecting children. From these people you can very quickly learn whom to contact in your state government and how best to go about accomplishing what you want.

Just as most state PTAs have a visible presence in their state capitals, so, too, the National PTA is active in Washington, where it tracks and analyzes legislation and regulations affecting children and youth; expresses the PTA's views formally through testimony before Congressional committees and regulatory bodies, and informally through frequent contacts with legislators and governmental staff; and helps individual parents find solutions to problems in their communities. Although its national headquarters is in Chicago, Illinois, the National PTA maintains an Office of Governmental Relations at 1201 16th Street NW, Washington, DC 20036. The National PTA issues a legislative newsletter called "What's Happening in Washington" that provides information on the status of issues before Congress and the executive and judicial branches of government. It also has a publication entitled *A Voice for Children and Youth: The National PTA Guide to Legislative Activities* that will provide you with information on how to communicate your views to policymakers as well as outline the legislative process.

If you have an issue you want to bring to the attention of state or federal policymakers, or if you want to register your views on a pending bill, you will need to do some research. Find out the pros and cons of the issue, who supports and opposes it, and whether existing or pending legislation already covers the issue. Find out if your state or the National PTA has already taken a position. Contact your state legislative chairman for advice and support. Talk to your local PTA members to get their views. Look for statistics and articles that back up your position, as well as surveys or opinion polls of parents and PTA members from your area or state. Then prepare a fact sheet with background information, names, addresses and phone numbers of supporters and agencies that deal with the issue and specific objectives that you wish to accomplish.

With this information, you are ready to contact policymakers. Direct, personal contact is one of the most effective ways to make your voice heard. To do this, call and ask for an appointment with the policymaker or an assistant who is handling the issue. If possible, arrange for other concerned parents to go to the meeting with you. Draft an agenda covering all the points you wish to discuss, and assign a role to each person who accompanies you. For example, one person can open the meeting and present the problem, another can report on parent and PTA views, and a third can be in charge of gathering and presenting supporting material. Be sure all the delegation arrives well before the appointment, and keep a careful watch on your time throughout the meeting.

Be open to questions. If you don't know the answer, offer to do additional research and get back to the questioner. After you have presented the issue and your views, ask how the member plans to vote or what the policymaker plans to do with your information. If the policymaker isn't ready to make a commitment, ask when you can call back for a decision. Remain polite even if you get a negative response to your request. Thank the policymaker for talking with you, since in time you may be able to accomplish your purpose if you develop a good working relationship. Once you contact a policymaker, stay in touch, monitoring the issue or issues that concern you, supplying new information, and thanking the policymaker or assistant for any support and assistance.

While meeting with and personally lobbying policymakers is most effective, letters, phone calls and the presentation of testimony are also useful. One letter may alert policymakers to your views, but many letters will show widespread concern for an issue. Therefore, you might want to consider starting a letter-writing campaign. Such a campaign also educates and involves the community, and publicizes your concerns.

Telegrams and phone calls can also be effective. If you decide to call a member of Congress, phone the legislator's district or Washington office and ask to speak to the legislator or an aide. Plan carefully in advance what you want to say and the actions you seek. Begin by stating that you are from the legislator's home district. Give a brief synopsis of your position and conclude by urging that the legislator support your position. You can increase the effectiveness of phone contacts if you mobilize a number of people to call.

Presenting testimony, whether to a state budget committee, a Congressional subcommittee or a Washington regulatory agency is another effective way to make your voice heard. Many committees invite individuals to testify, especially if they have become recognized experts on a topic. For more information about making your voice heard at the state or national level, contact your state PTA legislative chairman, state PTA office, state PTA president or the National PTA's Office of Governmental Relations.

A Nation at Risk

One area in which parents need to make their voices heard is in improving their local schools. For much of the last decade America has heard a great deal about the "excellence in education," or educational reform, movement. In 1983 the National Commission on Excellence in Education reported, "The educational foundations of our society are presently being eroded by a rising tide of mediocrity that threatens our very future as a Nation and a people. What was unimaginable a generation ago has begun to occur—others are matching and surpassing our educational attainments." The report, which the National Commission called *A Nation at Risk: The Imperative for Educational Reform,* touched off a fire storm of controversy in the political arena, the media and the educational community that has not quieted even after more than two dozen national reports from educational, governmental and business groups have studied nearly every aspect of education in America.

The National Commission based its call for educational

reform on disturbing data that had accumulated over the previous two decades, such as the declines from 1963 to 1981 in the SAT scores administered to college-bound high school students. In addition to the general downward trend, the percentage of students who scored at the top also fell dramatically. This awakened fears that in years to come America would not have enough scientists, intellectuals and leaders to compete in the world market.

Other tests of high school and younger students reported similar declines in achievement. For example, tests showed that 40 percent of high school students did not possess the higher-order thinking skills needed to solve complex math problems, to write a persuasive essay or to analyze material they have read or learned. As if this weren't bad enough, in tests administered during the 1970s to students in Japan, France, Germany, Sweden, Israel and England, among other countries, American students ranked far down on the list. In fact, American students came in dead last among the industrial countries in seven of nineteen tests.

Business leaders complained that high school graduates lacked basic skills in reading, writing and arithmetic, and that their companies had to spend millions of dollars teaching workers what they should have learned in school. The military reported a similar situation. The navy found that a quarter of its recent recruits couldn't read at the ninth-grade level.

The National Commission concluded that "the average graduate of our schools and colleges today is not as well-educated as the average graduate of 25 or 35 years ago." It blamed this decline on a weakening of school curriculum and high school graduation requirements. Where once most of students' time was spent on academic subjects—English, math, science and social sciences—42 percent of all students in 1979 were on a general education track in which a quarter of the credits were in P.E., health and such life-skills courses as marriage and family living. Even those students on an academic track to prepare for college took more electives in life-skills and general interest subjects. Approximately another 11 percent of high school students followed the vocational track and spent too much time in classes preparing for specialized jobs such as auto mechanic or typist rather than in math, science, English and other courses that would prepare them to hold different jobs over their lifetime.

The National Commission also cited other causes for the downward trend: the small amount of time spent on homework, grade inflation—the tendency for teachers to give more A's and B's for less accomplishment, a decline in the quality of teachers, the failure to keep good teachers in the classroom, the comparatively short American school year and the lack of clear goals in our schools.

The National Commission recommended a toughening of high school graduation requirements so that all students would receive adequate training in what it called the "five new basics." Specifically, it called for all high school graduates to have taken four years of English plus at least three years of mathematics, three years of science, three years of social studies and half a year of computer science. In addition, students planning to go to college were strongly advised to take two or more years of a foreign language.

To strengthen education further, the National Commission recommended that both the school day (now generally six hours long) and the school year (generally 180 days) be lengthened to seven hours a day and 200 to 220 days a year. It called for the better training, evaluation and higher salaries of teachers, and for the development of career ladders through which teachers could move from beginning instructor to experienced or master teacher, based on competence as well as experience. This would give teachers an incentive for improving their performance and keep the best of them in the classroom, the National Commission believed.

A Nation at Risk was not the first study calling for the

reform of education, but it was one of the most dramatic. The Reagan administration was anxious to spotlight the weaknesses of public education, and politicians in Washington and in state capitals around the nation quickly jumped on the bandwagon. Everyone agreed that something needed to be done to strengthen the schools, but few could decide what exactly should be done, how the reforms should be accomplished or where the money was to come from.

In the middle of the uproar over public education, two important books, based on years of research and study of American schools, were published by respected educators: John Goodlad's *A Place Called School* and *High School: A Report on Secondary Education in America,* by Ernest Boyer and the Carnegie Foundation for the Advancement of Teaching. Both provide an excellent understanding of problems facing education and possible solutions.

A number of recent reports have focused on teachers. While the SAT scores of all high school students have declined over the past few decades, the scores of those entering teaching have dipped even faster. Where once many of the brightest students (especially the brightest women) went into teaching, by the early 1980s the bulk of teachers was being drawn from the lower ranks of college students. Part of the reason for this change is that women now have many more career opportunities than they once did. At one time teaching was one of the most prestigious, attractive occupations for women, but today the brightest women are more likely to go into another profession.

Other factors make teaching less attractive than it once was. Throughout the 1960s and 1970s teacher salaries failed to keep up with inflation, so by the early 1980s teachers were among the lowest-paid college graduates. Also, at one time teaching was a highly respected profession. At the turn of the twentieth century, local teachers were looked up to as the best-educated members of their community. By the 1980s that respect had largely evaporated, as can be seen in the results of two Gallup polls. A 1969 poll found that 75 percent of Americans wanted their children to become teachers, but a 1983 poll showed that only 45 percent still did.

Many educational reform reports called for higher teacher salaries, for merit pay for outstanding teachers, for a career ladder, for testing of teachers to assess their knowledge of basic English and math, and for tougher college training of teachers. Not only teachers got attention. Many reports noted the critical role of the principal in shaping the school climate, and they recommended better training, evaluation and salaries for principals.

Curricula and teaching methods were investigated in great detail. Reports also criticized textbooks and teachers' increasing reliance on textbooks, workbooks and worksheets. Critics charged that over the past two decades textbook publishers have simplified textbooks—"dumbed them down," as one secretary of education called it. Fearful of controversy, the publishers have removed topics such as evolution and the role of religion in American history. Even more important, they have concentrated on making textbooks that are very easy to read rather than challenging. Lots of big pictures and colored boxes with a few facts or an anecdote have been woven around a small amount of very simple copy. California's superintendent of public instruction led the attack against "dumbed-down" textbooks by refusing to accept a number of texts for use in California schools until they were strengthened.

Another group of reports called for closer links between schools and business, and for changes in high school curricula to produce graduates better suited for employment. A final group of reports concentrated on students who drop out or otherwise fail to get an education that prepares them to be productive citizens. These students, called students at risk because they are at risk of failing in school, account for at least 30 percent of all students and a much higher percentage of minorities. The reforms called for in the first wave of reports weren't helping these students. In some cases, reform efforts such as a stiffer curriculum were making them fall farther behind and thus encouraged them to drop out.

Reform and Reality

After more than half a decade and dozens of reform proposals, no sweeping overhaul seems to be taking place in our nation's schools. So far it appears that reforms will be limited in scope and minor in effect. In fact, there may be little concrete change in your school. In a few places experiments are being tried that would make greater changes, but these are the exception.

The reform movement has focused attention on education at a time when most Americans have been taking their schools for granted. By spotlighting education, the reformers have put pressure on schools, principals and teachers to do their best. The reports and reformers have started parents and other citizens asking questions and paying more attention to education. All this has brought a new feeling of vitality to some schools and an awareness of the crucial role of education in shaping our nation's future.

Other concrete changes resulting from the reform movement can be found, but they don't add up to sweeping reform. More than forty states have toughened their high school graduation requirements. Teachers' salaries have been increased across much of the nation. Between 1983 and 1986, average teacher salaries increased 23 percent, according to the U.S. Department of Education, but in many areas compensation is still too low to attract and keep the best teachers.

In a few states, such as Tennessee, efforts have been made to create a career ladder for teachers, but career ladders have often been successfully opposed by teachers' unions. Some states have instituted competency exams to test prospective teachers or, in a few cases, those already in the classrooms. In some states a distressingly high number of prospective teachers, especially minority teachers, have failed, leading to charges that the tests are culturally biased against minorities. Also, critics charge that, while these tests measure what teachers don't know, they don't measure how well they teach.

Experiments are being carried out in Florida and in a few other areas to determine whether transferring some of the decision-making power from school boards, school districts and superintendents to individual schools and school-site councils will lead to higher achievement, greater teacher satisfaction and more parent involvement. These school-site councils, which often include the local principal, teacher representatives, parent representatives, community members and in many cases students, are part of a move to reform the nation's schools from the bottom up, rather than from the federal or state level down.

Some schools are attempting to improve the education they offer by increasing parent and community involvement. This is one of the cheapest, quickest and most effective ways to improve student achievement, so it is not surprising that many schools have seized on parent involvement as a panacea for all the ills of education. If schools really are committed to increasing parent involvement and if they succeed in this effort, they may realize that this is the most effective reform they can make.

To find out what has been happening in your school, talk to school leaders—the principal, your PTA president or a school board member. Ask what educational reforms your state has mandated and what changes the school has made. Ask your PTA to schedule a meeting to update parents on reform efforts.

Don't expect too much to have changed, though. In 1988, well into the educational reform movement, the Gallup/Phi

Delta Kappa Poll of the Public's Attitudes Toward the Public Schools found that only 29 percent of respondents thought the public schools in their community had improved over the last five years, 19 percent thought the schools were worse and 37 percent thought they had stayed the same. No noticeable tide of reform and improvement seems to be sweeping the nation.

Yet small changes are being made here and there. If enough small changes are made in enough communities this year and next year and in the years to come, improved education is possible in the 1990s. You can make a difference in your school, and together with millions of other Americans you can make a difference for all America's children.

Censorship Hurts Everyone

Educational reform is not the only issue that should concern parents today. Parents should also make their voices heard about what their children read. Monitor your child's reading material in the same way that you monitor the movies she attends and what she watches on TV. Become familiar with her textbooks and the other material she is assigned in school and the books she checks out of the library or buys at the bookstore. Note, however, that while you as a parent may have the right to decide what *your* child will and will not read, you have no right to decide what *other* children will read. When anyone, whether a parent or not, tries to ban a book or to insist that no student shall read it, this is censorship, and censorship hurts everyone.

Why is censorship harmful? Education should teach *how* to think—not *what* to think. It should develop young people's ability to evaluate a wide range of materials, views and experiences. Censorship denies students the right to explore ideas and to make informed, rational judgments. It also reduces their capacity to adjust to a changing world. As stated in *The Students' Right to Read,* a pamphlet issued by the

National Council of Teachers of English, "Censorship leaves students with an inadequate and distorted picture of ideals, values and problems of their culture . . . [and they are] denied the freedom to explore ideas and pursue truth wherever and however they wish."

Censorship has potentially devastating effects on our nation. From its founding, America has been a pluralist society, in which many viewpoints and cultures have coexisted and in which other people's views have been respected. Therefore, individuals and groups should not try to impose their beliefs and values on all children. According to Judith Krug, director of the American Library Association's Office for Intellectual Freedom, "Our democratic form of government runs on the basis of an enlightened electorate. Enlightenment comes from the ability to think and from exercising that ability across a broad spectrum of points of view, but censorship limits the ability of future voters and leaders to think."

Censorship of school material, texts and curriculum increased dramatically in the eighties. Previously most people who called for the exclusion of materials from schools and public libraries were concerned that these materials would harm their children. Today many parents still complain about words, ideas or subject matter that conflicts with their beliefs. Increasingly, though, censorship has become a tool of special-interest or extremist groups that want schools to be a place for inculcating youth with *their* political, social and religious views.

Many would-be censors charge that books used in school are un-American, anti-Christian, humanistic, Communistic, racist or in violation of what they call "traditional American values." Material that has been censored includes *The Catcher in the Rye, 1984, The Wizard of Oz, Huckleberry Finn, The Diary of Anne Frank, The Scarlet Letter, Moby Dick, Romeo and Juliet, National Geographic* and many of the books written by Judy Blume, a popular author of works for young people.

Textbook material has come under especially heavy at-

DECIDING WHAT YOUR CHILD MAY READ

• Be aware of what your child is reading. If she is young, go with her to the library and help select books. Read what she reads and discuss with her the books she is assigned in school. If you object to something she is reading, discuss this with her.

• Buy or check out of the library books that demonstrate your beliefs and values.

• If your child is assigned or has checked out a book that you fear may be objectionable, read the book—all of the book—not just selected parts.

• If after reading the book you still have concerns, discuss them with the teacher or librarian. Ask why the book was assigned or selected. What is its purpose? How will it be handled in class? How has it been received by the professional community and by other students?

• Do not automatically reject a book just because it contains something that shocks you, since the shocking section may serve a purpose. For example, a book about a young drug addict that contains bad language and graphic details may be very effective in showing youngsters the evils of drug use.

• Ask yourself if your child is really going to be harmed by what she reads. If not, trust her and let her read widely, but make it a point to discuss controversial books. As a general rule, if a book is too advanced for children, they won't read it. Conversely, if they can understand a book, they are probably ready for it. Before you forbid your child to read a book or type of book, ask yourself if you are overprotecting her. For example, are you trying to keep her from knowing about teen suicide, sexuality or drug use—when she will only learn about them elsewhere instead?

• If after reading a book, talking to the teacher and carefully thinking about the pros

tack. Topics most likely to be censored are American history, current events, sex education, science and discussions of the classes in society. Often extremists brand as un-American any material about our country they view as negative. Thus some groups are pressuring textbook publishers and schools to eliminate any references to slavery, the civil rights movement, Watergate, Vietnam War protests and controversial questions such as whether the United States should have bombed Hi-

and cons, you decide that your child should not read the book, explain your position and ask the teacher to assign another book for your child to read. State your objections in clear, unemotional terms. Don't call the book "filthy" or "trash," since your "trash" may be someone else's prizewinner. Teachers will almost always comply with a parent's request and assign a different book.

• Remember, too, that while you have the right to limit what your child reads, you don't have the right to impose your views on others. A book that you find objectionable may be perfectly acceptable to another parent, so consider carefully before asking that all class members be prohibited from reading it.

• If you strongly object to a book, ask to file a formal complaint, but be aware that this may turn a seldom-read book into an instant bestseller and thus publicize the very views you oppose.

• Remember that no one really wins a censorship battle, since censorship is a harmful practice that destroys ideas and limits the development of youngsters' thinking ability. Also remember that if you set a precedent and ban from your school or public library a book that you believe is objectionable, someday soon someone may censor a book or view that you hold dear. And, as the American Library Association's Judith Krug has said, "If all people had the right to censor every book that they didn't like, soon there would be nothing left on the library shelves for our children to read."

• If you feel strongly about maintaining the freedom to read, oppose censorship attempts in your community and nationwide. Offer to assist your school and community library in the selection process and in community education. Contact the American Library Association's Office for Intellectual Freedom, 50 East Huron Street, Chicago, IL 60611 to find out what else you can do.

roshima. Also, some extremists insist that works must portray women only in what they call their "traditional roles as wives and mothers," minimize or eliminate discussion of ethnic and racial groups, and reflect only the narrowest of Judeo-Christian religious views.

To give parents a say in what their children read as well as to prevent censorship problems, all schools should have a written policy on the selection of textbooks, library books and other material. To be most effective, the selection process should include a committee made up of school staff and parents. In addition, the school should have a formal complaint procedure, allowing the filing of an objection against use of material. The National Council of Teachers of English, the American Library Association and the National School Boards Association have sample selection and complaint policies that can be adapted to the needs of your individual school. If your school district lacks either of these policies, strongly urge that they be developed before a problem occurs.

Schools should inform parents and the community of both selection and complaint procedures and of any censorship threats. They should also involve parents in the selection and review process. No action should be taken unless a formal complaint is filed against a book or other material. If a complaint is filed, the material should be left on the shelves or in use until the complaint is fairly and carefully considered according to the established guidelines. In evaluating whether to keep or remove a book or other material, parents should remember the words of Supreme Court Justice William Brennan, who wrote in the Supreme Court decision overturning a censorship attempt in Island Tree, New York, that a school board may exclude books which are "pervasively vulgar" or lack "educational suitability," but that "local school boards may not remove books from the library shelves simply because they dislike the ideas contained in those books and seek by their removal to prescribe what shall be orthodox in politics, nationalism, religion or other matters of opinion."

Generally, students do best when they are encouraged to read as widely as possible and when they are provided with values and experiences at home that allow them to evaluate this material critically. Therefore, the National PTA has joined the battle to prevent censorship in several recent cases heard by the Supreme Court, and it has opposed the efforts of special-interest groups to insist on the teaching of their beliefs. It has called on parents and PTAs across the nation to support the right of students to read, while protecting the right of individual parents to decide what their own children will and will not read.

PTAs in Action

Here are a few examples of PTAs that have been effective in helping parents make their voices heard:

- Since 1973 the president and vice president of each PTA in Salt Lake City, Utah, have served on committees that work with school administrators to make decisions for the schools. All school districts in Salt Lake City have such school community councils, which, working within the board's guidelines and budget, determine the educational needs, develop annual school goals, evaluate discipline methods and set the daily school schedule. Besides the PTA officials, other parents, community members and teacher representatives also serve on the councils. As parent involvement in decision making has increased in Salt Lake City, so has student achievement.
- When the Nevada State Legislature passed Proposition 6, which would have slashed state funding for schools, Las Vegas PTA leaders swung into action. According to state law, such a proposition must pass the voters twice. It swept through the first time before the PTA got organized, but once local and state PTAs studied the proposal and spelled out clearly what it would mean for the schools, the voters defeated the proposition the second time around by 75 percent.
- The R. D. Head PTA in Lilburn, Georgia, made its voice heard in another way. PTA members were very concerned about child abuse, so the PTA organized a campaign to build an emergency shelter for abused children. The PTA prepared a slide show outlining the problem, enlisted the support of nineteen community organizations, educated the community

and raised $227,000 from grants and private contributions for the shelter.

- Atlanta's D. M. Therrel High School PTSA felt that, given the known health risks of cigarette smoking, its school was wrong to have designated a smoking area for students. The PTA took the issue to the school board. Despite considerable opposition, the board established a policy that prohibits students from smoking on any of the schoolgrounds of Atlanta's public schools.
- Washington Village PTA leaders in Washington, Vermont, were worried about the effects of federal and state budget cuts on their schools, so they scheduled a meeting to discuss the cuts and suggested ways to recoup the losses. Though a small PTA in a rural area, it sent members to monitor the state legislature and to provide testimony at hearings about the educational budget and other topics affecting the lives of children.
- Parents at the Geronimo Road Post School in Fort Sill, Oklahoma, felt their children were being shortchanged because their school library was out of date and lacked a librarian. They went to their PTA for help. With support from families and school staff, the PTA convinced the school board that library improvement must be made a budget priority. In addition, a parent who was studying to become a librarian helped the school apply for a state grant to improve the library.
- Parents in Hunterdon County, New Jersey, were deeply disturbed when they learned that their school buildings contained asbestos. The school district called for a referendum to obtain funds to remove this cancer-causing material, but the community defeated it by five votes. Then the Union Township PTA began a drive to educate the public about the dangers of asbestos. Members campaigned door to door, held a public forum and supported the referendum when it was put back on the ballot the next year. With PTA and parent support, the referendum passed resoundingly.

• The Northeast Council of PTA in Chicago, the Moon Mountain PTA in Phoenix, Arizona, the Salt Lake City PTA Council in Utah and the Safari PTA in Chanute, Kansas, were among the PTAs that conducted surveys of their schools using the National PTA's *Looking in on Your School* brochure. These PTAs found areas that needed to be improved as well as strengths that had been unrecognized. They worked with their local school boards, administrators and teachers to translate what they learned into positive changes for students in their community.

• Although the temperature often soars well into the upper nineties in San Antonio, Texas, most schools weren't air-conditioned until the San Antonio City PTA Council launched a "PTA Supports Cool Schools!" campaign. Parents were mobilized to pass a referendum earmarking funds for much-needed school air conditioning.

• Members of the Smoketree PTA in Lake Havasu City, Arizona, recognized that their school needed a lunch program. Because the school district was unwilling or unable to undertake such a program, the PTA organized and operated a five-day-a-week lunch program for students in their school.

• The Lambertville PTA in Lambertville, New Jersey, tried to convince its school board that art education was an important part of a child's education, but the board said it had no money for an art teacher. The PTA then developed a resource pool of artists who could come into the schools to teach basic art as well as such art-related topics as calligraphy and puppetry.

• The PTAs in Howard County, Maryland, have been very successful over the last decade in helping parents make their voices heard. A recent profile in the *Columbia Flier/Howard County Times* saluted the PTA for "staving off efforts to hold down school spending and gradually winning support for smaller class sizes, health aides in the elementary schools, better programs for gifted students and more."

CHAPTER

10

Why Care About Other People's Children?

YOU SEE THEIR faces on the nightly news—homeless children living in welfare hotels in New York, in the back seats of autos in California and in temporary shelters in Chicago. Most of us think of the homeless as aging bag ladies, recently released mental patients, drug addicts or adults who won't or can't find work and housing. So we're shocked when we learn that the fastest-growing group of homeless in America are children. More than 100,000 children in the United States have no home. Most live in our large cities and attend school only irregularly, if at all. Many slip totally through the cracks in our education system, spending their lives on the streets or in tiny run-down rooms.

If you're like most parents, when you see these children on television, you think, "Isn't that awful! Something should be done about it. It will never happen to my child, thank goodness." Then you go about your daily business—certain that, no matter how sad, homeless children won't affect you or your child's lives.

The same thing probably happens when you read other shocking statistics. Today nearly one quarter of all children under six live in poverty. In the 1960s it was considered a national disgrace that almost one third of older Americans were spending their last years in poverty. Today the poverty rate for seniors is down to 14 percent, but the poverty rate for children under the age of six has shot up from 14 percent in the late 1960s to over 25 percent. Almost half of all the poor in the United States are children.

Since poverty goes hand in hand with many other problems, almost one quarter of all American children live in families that are likely to experience poor housing, poor health care, poor nutrition, the continuing threats of violence and drugs, and few expectations for a brighter tomorrow. Many of these children living in poverty can look forward to a poor education as well. Still, these problems seem far away to most of us.

Then there are the statistics on teenage pregnancy. America has the highest rate of teenage pregnancy of any developed nation. Each year more than 1.1 million teenage girls get pregnant. About half of them have babies, and half of those who do are not married at the time they give birth. When an unmarried teenager has a baby, there are profound effects on two generations. Babies born to teenage mothers are much more likely to have a low birth weight, to be mentally or physically handicapped, to be slow developers or to die at birth. Approximately 80 percent of teenage mothers drop out of school, and most never go back. A high percentage of these mothers and babies live on welfare—subsisting on little money, with no job prospects and little hope for a better life. In many cases, in spite of their best intentions, these "children having children" are unprepared and unable to be good parents.

The grim statistics never seem to stop. It is estimated that as many as 27 percent of all students, or approximately 1 million students a year, drop out before they finish high school. Those students most at risk live in cities, are poor and come from minority groups. The dropout rate for blacks is almost twice as high as for whites, and approximately 45 percent of all Hispanic students drop out of school. In large cities the dropout rate for Native Americans may be as high as 85 percent, for Hispanics 75 percent and for blacks 50 percent. One study found that over 50 percent of all students in Chicago public schools drop out before graduation. Again, although these figures are disturbing, you may ask, "What has this got to do with my child, his education or his future? Can't we let Congress, educators, social service agencies and the PTA worry about this?" The answer is no!

"The children living 1,000 miles away, going to inadequate schools or spending their days in homeless shelters and not attending school at all, those dropping out or finishing school and not able to find jobs, or those children having children—they are the people who will one day fill your children's world," says Manya Ungar, former National PTA president. "What affects those children affects your children's lives directly or indirectly. If the poor, the homeless and disadvantaged children don't get the education and help they need, your children and our entire nation will suffer."

Children at Risk

The groups most likely to be termed "at risk" are children of poverty, children from minority groups, children from lower social and economic classes, children from non-English-speaking families, and teen mothers and their children. While there are heavy concentrations of children at risk in cities, they are found in rural areas or small towns as well. Not surprisingly, many of these groups overlap. Statistics indicate that if you belong to a minority group or are from a non-English-speaking family, you are more likely to live in poverty, drop out of school, have a teenage pregnancy and be a single parent. It is estimated that at least 30 percent of all elementary and high school students are at risk, and it is predicted that this percentage will increase rapidly.

Much of the initial education reform movement ignored

children at risk, concentrating instead on helping middle class students attain excellence. Until recently little attention was paid to those who are failing or barely squeaking by. Some of the education reforms (for example, requiring a more academic curriculum and instituting minimum competency exams for promotion or graduation) may even have worsened conditions, in the short run, for children at risk. Students already on the verge of dropping out may be pushed out because they can't meet the higher requirements. Likewise, if they fail a minimum competency exam after twelve years of substandard education, they may be given a certificate of attendance instead of a diploma, and pushed out to try to find jobs as best they can.

In the long run, strengthening high school graduation requirements and toughening the curriculum may help children at risk, but only if they are helped early in life and throughout their entire schooling. For the immediate future, though, many of these children will fail.

Dropouts and children at risk have begun to get more attention in the last few years, in part because business and industry have become concerned about what it is costing society to have teens leave school with few of the skills needed for work or to be fully participating citizens. Approximately one quarter of dropouts between the ages of sixteen and twenty-four are unemployed—a much higher percentage than of those who finish high school. Many more are not on the unemployment rolls because they are not actively looking for work. A study reported in Harriet Willis's *Students at Risk* found that a male student who dropped out of school in California would earn $187,000 less over his lifetime than a high school graduate, while a female dropout would earn $122,000 less. Thus, one class from a large urban high school with a 40-percent dropout rate, would lose millions of dollars in lifetime earnings. The Committee for Economic Development, composed of leaders from two hundred major American corporations, estimates that each year's school dropouts cost the nation $240 billion in lost earnings and taxes over their lifetime. To these billions of dollars must be added the high costs of welfare, law enforcement, crime and social services needed by the dropouts.

So a high national and local dropout rate costs America today and in the future. You and your children are going to pay heavily for the welfare and services extended to these dropouts at the same time that our economy suffers from their lost earnings.

A Changing America

The dropout rate and other problems become even more serious when you realize that the groups with the highest dropout rates, the highest poverty rates and the highest incidence of teen pregnancy are also the groups that are growing the fastest in America.

Today America's population is rapidly getting older, with the 70 million baby boomers born between 1946 and 1964 heading into middle age. Most baby boomers are white and, as Harold Hodgkinson reported in *All One System,* they have a much lower birthrate (1.7 children per white woman) than did their parents (who had a 2.9-per-white-woman birthrate). On the other hand, minority birthrates are 2.4 per woman for blacks and 2.9 for Mexican-Americans.

Immigration is also shifting the composition of American society. Hodgkinson's study shows that approximately two thirds of immigrants in the entire world are coming to the United States. Most of these immigrants to America are from the Hispanic areas of Mexico, Central and South America, or else from Asia. In 1988, a little over one in five Americans was a member of a minority group, but by the early twenty-first century the ratio will be one in three. Since the new immigrants are more likely to settle in California and in the

Southwest, as well as in our large cities, the minority population of these areas—already well above the national average—is expected to increase rapidly. Today California's elementary schools are composed of more than 50 percent minority students, and it is estimated that by the year 2010, minorities will comprise more than 50 percent of the entire state's population. Minority students also account for more than 45 percent of Texas schoolchildren, and in our twenty-five largest cities, over 50 percent of the children in public schools are from minority groups.

This is especially important for you and your children, because minorities are much more likely to be at risk, to live in poverty, to drop out of school or receive an inadequate education, and to have high unemployment, teen pregnancy and crime rates. So the number of children at risk within our society—those with high levels of economic, social and educational problems—is increasing rapidly, while the percentage of those most likely to succeed is shrinking.

An analysis of these statistics shows that something has to be done, and quickly. Already America has developed an underclass—what a 1986 *Education Week* report called "an underdeveloped country of some 40 million people—the minority of [whose] inhabitants are poor, nonwhite, uneducated if not illiterate, unemployed and often unemployable, and largely dependent on government for their survival." If this is not bad enough, the situation is going to worsen rapidly. As the report concludes, "The United States can no longer afford to waste a sixth or more of its human resources if the nation is to prosper and succeed."

Here is one more reason why you should care about children at risk. Harold Hodgkinson observes that, while in his father's day seventeen workers paid the social security for each person who retired, by 1992 there will be only three workers (in a rapidly aging America) to pay for social security, and one of those workers will come from an at-risk group.

Those disadvantaged children today will as adults help pay for your retirement as well as share the world with your children.

According to former National PTA President Ann Kahn, "The first thing that must be done is for all Americans, parents and nonparents alike, from all classes and backgrounds to recognize the problem of children at risk and to determine to help these children. We've denied the problem for too many years, but we can't ignore it any longer. It isn't just the matter of children suffering, which of course is terrible. It's a matter of our entire nation suffering. These children's success or failure will have a profound impact on the success or failure of America in the twenty-first century. I find one of the most frustrating things about the problem is that we do know ways to help; we just aren't doing it."

Government and private efforts were begun to help children at risk in the late 1960s and 1970s, and to a large extent they worked. For example, 40 percent of the reading gap between black and white children was eliminated in the 1970s alone, according to a report by the National Coalition of Advocates for Students. The gap could have been totally eliminated in the 1990s, the report says, except that government funds were slashed in the 1980s. The continuing cutback in funds means that today more than half of all students who need help to catch up in school never get any, and the help that is given is usually piecemeal.

Owen Butler, a retired chairman of Procter & Gamble and a leader of the Committee for Economic Development, testified before a congressional committee late in 1987 that education could wipe out poverty and most of its accompanying ills in one generation. According to Butler, a one-percent increase in local, state and federal taxes could pay for a comprehensive attack on poverty, with much of the funding and programs being channeled through the public schools. The Committee for Economic Development recommends a funding increase for Head Start, which provides disadvantaged three- to five-year-olds with a solid preschool learning experience as well as with health and social assistance. Even those critical of antipoverty programs concede that Head Start has been successful, but still the program has never received enough money to reach more than 20 percent of those eligible.

While most experts agree that a major program of preschool education would be one of the most effective ways to break the cycle of poverty, much more is needed. Mothers at the poverty level need better prenatal care; training in nutrition, good parenting and ways to stimulate their children; and jobs that pay enough to support their children and themselves. Schools serving the poor and disadvantaged need to be strengthened. In many cases all aspects of those schools need to be improved—from the dirty, crumbling and depressing buildings to the outdated educational materials and textbooks, to the quality of teachers, to the curriculum. A whole new spirit is needed in many of these schools, too—a spirit of hope and the expectation that all children can and will learn. This is important, because if teachers feel that children at risk really cannot learn, this becomes a self-fulfilling prophecy.

Remedial education programs must be increased or improved in elementary schools. Children can't be allowed to fall behind even in the first grade, because once they do, the lag will become more pronounced with each passing year. It may take a major restructuring of the way we teach, as well as smaller class sizes and classes built around material to be learned rather than age groupings, to allow teachers to develop more individualized instruction and to assure that all children succeed. In addition, more tutors are needed. Some of the most effective ones are already in the classroom—the peer tutors, or students who tutor others. They are especially well suited to working with children at risk.

Elementary school children must learn to read, write and do math. One step in this direction may well be to end tracking and ability grouping and to insist that all children learn the same basic material, no matter how long it takes and how much help they need. With a solid, basic foundation, children at risk will be better prepared for high school and for coping with a demanding academic curriculum rather than being shunted off into vocational education tracks. At the high school level, we must provide many more remedial programs to help students who are still having trouble.

While educators differ on the best way to help non-English speakers learn English, they all agree that students will not be able to succeed in school unless they become fluent in English. Today only about 10 percent of the estimated 2.7 million children from non-English-speaking backgrounds receive bilingual education, and only about one third receive any special assistance with English.

More programs are needed to help potential dropouts, who show signs of being at risk as early as first and second grades. The main cause of dropping out is failure to do well in school, usually combined with increasing absenteeism for boys and often with teen pregnancy for girls. Students must be helped to succeed in school, teenage mothers must be kept in school, parents and schools must work together to see that all students attend school regularly, potential dropouts must be encouraged to continue in school and those who have already dropped out must be helped to return to school.

In order to help children at risk, parents and schools must truly work together. Some parents of children at risk are already deeply involved in their children's education. Many of these parents, who see education as the only way out of a life of poverty, help their children succeed just by showing that education is important to them and by helping their children as much as possible at home. Unfortunately, though, too many parents of children at risk don't recognize the importance of education and of taking an active role in their children's education, don't know how to help their children or don't have enough energy and hope to work with them. Therefore, schools must actively reach out to these parents and help them work with their children at home.

"Two key elements underlie everything that needs to be done for children at risk," says Millie Waterman, a former National PTA vice president for legislative activity. "These elements are *will* and *dollars*. As a nation we must decide that we're going to help these children, and then we must spend the money to do it." Research has shown that for every dollar spent on early childhood education, the nation saves between four and seven dollars in remedial education, law enforcement, welfare, unemployment and other costs, and a similar payoff comes from other programs. "So it's a matter of pay now or pay much more later," Waterman continues. "The decision to ignore this problem and pay later will greatly influence your children's future and yours, too."

PTAs in Action

The National PTA has long been interested in reaching out to parents of children at risk. It has translated many of its important brochures into Spanish and provided funding to a number of urban PTAs through its "Big City Schools Project." Many local, council and state PTAs are working to get parents of at-risk children involved in their education. In addition, they provide direct help to children at risk. Here are some examples:

- The Tenth and Thirty-first District PTAs in Los Angeles used funding from the Big City Schools Project to translate brochures into several languages and to encourage minority parents to become active in their children's education.
- The Ninth District PTA in San Diego used funds from

the Big City Schools Project to determine how the needs of Hispanic, Asian and black parents could be more effectively addressed.

• The Dade County PTA Council in Florida used National PTA funds to help develop a series of cable TV programs in English and Spanish that provided information to PTA and community members, along with training for PTA leaders.

• The San Jose Council PTA in California has translated material for parents into Vietnamese, Spanish and Portuguese.

• The California State PTA has developed an "Hispanic Outreach Program," in cooperation with the South West Regional Education Lab, that shows Hispanic parents how to be involved in their children's education.

• The Magnolia High School PTA in Anaheim, California, serves a school with families from sixty-seven different countries. To reach all these families, it designated its open house week as "International Week" and planned parades, dinners and programs to share information about different cultures and customs.

• Many PTAs have been organized in Hispanic areas. The Leyndecker Elementary PTA in Laredo, Texas, which serves a school that is 99 percent Hispanic, conducts most of its meetings in Spanish but holds bilingual meetings when it knows that English speakers will be attending. Each month the PTA schedules a meeting on a topic of interest to parents, such as drug abuse prevention, discipline, child abuse, school testing or bilingual education. School administrators attend and keep parents informed about what is happening at school.

• In recent years, many PTAs, especially in urban areas, have noted a change in membership as minority groups begin to move into their areas. This change has meant that PTAs must adapt if they are to serve these new parents. One PTA that has adapted is the Cantara Street PTA in Reseda, California. In 1986, 68 percent of the parents in the Cantara

Street School were Hispanic and Spanish-speaking, but the PTA was predominantly Anglo and English-speaking. Therefore, PTA leaders decided to reach out more actively to Hispanic parents, involving them more closely in their children's education and in the PTA. An all-out effort resulted in a major increase in Hispanic members and in the sharing of PTA leadership among Anglos and Hispanics.

• Another PTA that has successfully adapted is the Lincolnwood PTA in Lincolnwood, Illinois, which serves Greek, Korean, Russian, Filipino, Indian and Anglo families. At the start of a recent school year, the PTA decided to send a member to welcome each of these families, deliver information about the school and the PTA, and encourage parents to participate in their school. Later in the year it assembled a panel of foreign-born parents to tell about their native customs, traditions and holidays, and conducted an ethnic festival with displays, songs, stories and food from twenty-eight different countries.

• The Lynn Road Elementary School PTA in Raleigh, North Carolina, organized volunteers—parents, teachers, community members—to work with children at risk. Volunteers tutored the students once a week and made at least one other weekly contact with them also.

• The District of Columbia PTA Congress has for many years had a "Shoe and Rubber Fund." Each year the PTA receives between $35,000 and $50,000 in funding from United Way, which it supplements with money from its local PTAs and other sources. Parents of children who need shoes, boots or rubbers can ask their school's guidance counselor or principal for assistance. Teachers who notice students needing footwear can tell the guidance counselor. Parents are then provided with tickets allowing them to get shoes for their children at several local stores.

• The D.C. PTA Congress and many local units in the District of Columbia also have what they call "student aid rooms," where needy students can get clothing. The local PTAs hold "bundle days" to collect clothing that has been outgrown but not worn out.

• The Springfield PTA Council in Springfield, Oregon, works with local PTAs, Goodwill Industries, United Way and local businesses to raise money and collect clothing for needy children.

• The Creston School PTA in Portland, Oregon, sponsored a canned food drive for the needy. As part of the project it showed a family movie and charged admission of one can of food per person.

• To help dependent and delinquent youth, the California State PTA organized in 1983 the Contra Costa County Court School PTA. This PTA serves about four hundred youngsters in juvenile centers and children's shelters, as well as incarcerated adults who want to finish their schooling. It works directly with students, providing volunteers to tutor and counsel them.

• The 6th District PTA in the San Fernando Valley in California supports a health and dental clinic in cooperation with the Los Angeles Unified School District. Any child can get a complete physical for a minimal cost. Local PTAs pay for the children's care if families can't. The center, which has been in operation for more than forty years, receives United Way funding.

NOW THAT YOU know how to become more involved in your child's education and school, it is time to draw up concrete plans for getting her the best education possible. Following are suggestions for actions you can take, grouped into categories based on goals. For example, you may decide that you want to improve your child's reading, or help her more with homework, or become more actively involved in your school. After reading through this section, choose one or two goals to work on right away, and agree with your child on several actions that will help move toward those goals.

Using the suggested ideas and some of your own, make a chart of your intentions. In the following sample action plan, you will find a chart that you can fill out with your own action plan. A word of advice—select a reasonable number of activities, but also set up a long-range plan for adding more when you and your child feel comfortable with the new routine. Don't try to do everything at once, because you may get so overwhelmed that you do nothing. On the other hand, don't be satisfied with deciding to do only one or two activities. Probably your long-range goal should be to begin working *this* year on all the suggested areas in which you or your child is weak.

SAMPLE ACTION PLAN

I will do the following:

Goal	Action	How Often
1. Help Elisabeth read	Read to her twenty minutes	Nightly
	Subscribe to two magazines for her	Yearly
	Limit TV to an hour	Nightly
	Take her to the library	Weekly
2. Build self-esteem	Talk with her thirty minutes	Nightly
	Praise her for being good	Nightly
	Don't yell at her	Daily

You may want to duplicate and fill out charts for each child or to combine your plans into one chart. When you have finished your plans, why not transfer them to a chart to be hung in your kitchen, to remind you of the actions needed to assure your child the best possible education? And be sure to put suggested times for various actions. When you lead a busy life, often things don't get done unless you schedule them and then keep carefully to that schedule.

POSSIBLE GOALS AND ACTIONS

1. To improve my child's reading ability and help her enjoy reading:

- Read to my child.
- Listen to her read aloud or read jointly—taking turns reading to each other.
- Take my child to the library.
- Establish a family reading time.
- Help my child with a writing project, such as writing a story or keeping a diary.
- Subscribe to magazines that will interest her.

- Buy or check out of the library books about her interests.
- Set up a reading program with an agreed-upon schedule of books to be read, and give rewards (stickers or special treats) for meeting goals.
- Set a good example—let my child see me reading for enjoyment.
- Limit television watching.

2. To stimulate my child's interest in learning:

- Plan family activities that are both educational and fun, such as trips to museums and nature walks.
- Play games, do puzzles.
- Set aside fifteen minutes a day to discuss school and her activities.
- Talk with her about anything and everything, especially about what interests her.
- Let my child know how much I value education, how education or the lack of education has influenced my life, and the importance of getting a good education for her future.
- Make my child aware that I want her to do her very best in school but not apply undue pressure to achieve.
- Avoid sex-stereotyping my child by telling her that "girls aren't good at math" or that "most boys don't like foreign languages."
- Praise my child for a job well done, whether for finishing her homework at night or bringing home a good score on a test.
- Allow plenty of time for her to play, since children learn a great deal from play.

3. To limit television and its negative effects:

- Decide upon the amount of TV that can be watched.
- Set the hours when the TV can be on or must be turned off.

- Select in advance with my child those programs our family will watch.
- Watch TV with my child, discuss with her what we see on TV and ask questions that make her think about what she is watching.
- Explain to her the purpose of commercials and how TV action is faked.
- Limit the amount of violence my child watches and discuss violence with her.
- Turn the TV off after the programs we have selected are over.
- Set a good example—limit *my* television time, too.

4. To build my child's self-esteem:

- Make time for my child—spend time alone talking to, listening to and playing with her.
- Praise her for accomplishments, for helping and for good behavior.
- Have reasonable expectations for my child and help her set "do-able" goals.
- Be careful not to put too much pressure on her to succeed.
- Eliminate negative and hurtful comments.
- Help her learn to deal with peer pressure.
- Hug and kiss my child, and show her that she is loved and respected.
- Avoid sex-stereotyping my child.
- Treat my child as I would my friends.
- Set a good example—feel good about myself.
- Evaluate my discipline techniques and work on building my child's feelings of self-worth along with her self-discipline.

5. To help my child become self-disciplined:

- Set limits but make only those rules that are absolutely necessary and that will be enforced.

- Give her responsibility, and acknowledge and praise her for completing chores or otherwise taking responsibility.
- Encourage independence, such as by letting my child make her own decisions.
- Make sure my child understands rules, and allow her to help make them as she gets older.
- Explain to her the consequences of actions, and teach her that she will have to be responsible for what she does.

6. To help my child with schoolwork at home:

- Set up a quiet place for her to study, with all necessary supplies close at hand.
- Establish a time for homework when I or another adult is available to help, or set up a reading time if my child is too young for homework.
- Help my child develop good study habits, including not studying in front of the TV.
- Suggest or help my child make a homework calendar or an assignment notebook.
- Look over her homework each night, dating and signing it if she goes to elementary school.
- Review returned homework with her.
- Congratulate or praise my child for doing well on homework and for working hard.
- Consider getting a tutor, either an adult or peer tutor, or some other special help if my child needs more assistance than I can give.

7. To monitor my child's progress in school:

- Set up a file for each child into which I put exams, papers, returned homework and grade cards, and review the files regularly.
- Discuss grade cards with my child, looking for something to praise and any trends which indicate potential trouble.

- Encourage her to do her best in all classes, including math, science, art and physical education.
- Check to be sure that I am not putting too much pressure on my child to succeed.
- Call the teacher or send a note about any problems or questions with homework or school.
- Learn about the school curriculum, look at textbooks and be aware of what is being taught and happening in school.
- Attend all parent-teacher conferences.
- Check and correct if necessary my child's school records.
- Learn what, why and when tests are to be given.
- Understand my child's test results and find out what her teachers plan to do with them.
- Keep an eye on my child's out-of-school schedule to see that she isn't working too many hours, or that sports or other activities aren't taking too much time away from studying and play.

8. To become more involved in my child's education and her school:

- Get to know my child's teachers.
- Develop a close working relationship with those teachers.
- Call teachers as soon as problems arise.
- Thank teachers for any special assistance and for a job well done.
- Learn about the school's homework policy and monitor my child's homework.
- Discuss school rules and regulations with my child, and be sure that she knows I support school rules.
- See that my child attends school every day unless she is ill, and let her know that I will not tolerate her skipping school.
- Obtain a copy of the school's discipline policy, read and understand it and other school rules and regulations.
- Attend school concerts, open houses and ball games in

which my child participates, and attend other school events with her.

- As much as my schedule allows, volunteer in the school or help with school activities in other ways.
- Join, attend and become active in my PTA.

9. To get help for my child's special needs:

- If my child is handicapped, see that she is properly evaluated.
- Attend and take an active part in all eligibility and IEP (individualized education program) planning meetings.
- Monitor how the IEP is carried out.
- Assure that she is getting all possible help.
- Be certain that my child is placed in the least restrictive environment and that she is mainstreamed for at least part of the day, if possible.
- If my child is gifted, see about getting special help to challenge her and help her achieve her potential.
- Provide special help or challenge at home and in the community for my child whether she is handicapped or gifted.

10. To keep my child healthy and safe:

- Be sure my child has regular physical checkups and receives good care for all illnesses and accidents, paying particular attention to her vision and hearing.
- See that she gets plenty of nutritious food and lots of rest.
- Encourage my child to get vigorous exercise—play with her and help her find sports and other activities that she will enjoy.
- Plan vigorous family activities, such as swimming, soccer or jogging.
- Be sure that my child knows how to swim.
- Check on the physical education offered at my school—

children need a period of vigorous physical activity each day.

- Be sure that my child is adequately supervised after school—check on school-age child care and be sure that she knows how to keep herself safe if she is at home alone.
- Help my child learn to deal with peer pressure, to make decisions, weigh options and understand consequences.
- Be alert for the warning signs of suicide, and get immediate help if my youngster needs it.
- Help my child learn to deal with stress.
- Teach my child to express her feelings.
- Be sure that my school offers good health education classes taught by trained, experienced teachers.
- Insist that school health education include information on topics such as sexuality, AIDS, sexually transmitted diseases, alcohol and drug abuse prevention, physical fitness, accident prevention, smoking and mental health.
- Talk to my child about important issues like sexuality, AIDS, drugs and alcohol, values and beliefs.

11. To prevent problems with sex and AIDS:

- Be sure that my child gets a good sex education at home and in school, tell her my values and teach her to take responsibility for her own sexuality.
- Help my teenage son or daughter (who may be sexually active) to understand how to prevent unwanted pregnancies and not to take advantage of others.
- Talk to my child about AIDS—how it is spread and how it is not spread—and how she can protect herself.
- Check to be sure that my school has an AIDS policy that protects students, staff and teachers as well as preserves the rights of any child or staff member who may have AIDS.
- Be sure that, while my school's sex education curriculum encourages delaying of sexual activity, it also provides ad-

equate information and assistance for those young people who decide not to wait.

- Talk about date rape and how to prevent it with my son as well as daughter.

12. To prevent abuse of alcohol and other drugs:

- Know the facts about alcohol and drug abuse, and talk with my child about them often, beginning when she is very young.
- Let her know my rules about alcohol and drugs as well as what is legal and illegal.
- Recognize that alcohol is a drug, that it is illegal for young people under twenty-one to drink; and do not tolerate its use any more than that of other drugs.
- Don't allow my child to attend parties where alcohol or other drugs will be served or where parents are not present.
- Know where my child is at all times, whom she is with and what she is doing.
- Do not allow alcohol or drugs to be used by youngsters at any parties at my home.
- Set a good example by using alcohol wisely, if at all, by not using illegal drugs or abusing those that are legal and by not smoking.
- Strongly encourage my child not to start smoking and to stop if she has already begun.
- Check on my school's alcohol prevention and enforcement plan as well as rules relating to smoking at school.

13. To improve education for my child and all the children in my community:

- Learn who my school board members are.
- Vote in all school elections, attend school board meetings and candidate nights.

- Make my views known on issues related to my child's school and education.
- Evaluate school policies such as the discipline code and suggest needed changes (for example, the abolition of corporal punishment).
- Work with other parents to study the school budget and to review school priorities and long-range plans.
- Organize parents to secure needed services and school improvements.
- Check on my school's textbook selection policy, and offer to serve on the book selection or other committees.
- Work to see that there is school-age child care available to families in my school and that my child is adequately supervised after school.

14. To affect educational policy locally, statewide and nationally:

- Monitor the efforts of my school district and state to improve education, and suggest other ideas that could be tried.
- Assure that adequate funding is provided by local, state and federal governments.
- Write or call my state legislators and members of Congress to make my opinions known and to support strengthening of public education locally, statewide and nationally.
- Insist that adequate programs (for example, dropout prevention projects, early childhood education, remedial and bilingual education, prenatal and postnatal health care) be available to help at-risk students and others achieve their full potential.
- Work to see that all children—girls and boys, average, gifted and handicapped, rich and poor—get the help they need.
- Support public education, which is the bulwark of our democracy.

Now you know what needs to be done, and you have ideas about where to begin. You can improve your child's schools. You can get the best possible education for your child and for all America's children. The National PTA is ready to help you, as it has been for more than ninety years, because our children are our greatest national resource—and our future.

MY ACTION PLAN

I will do the following:

Goal	**Action**	**How Often** (daily, weekly, monthly, other)
1. ________	________	____
	________	____
	________	____
	________	____
	________	____
2. ________	________	____
	________	____
	________	____
	________	____
	________	____
	________	____
3. ________	________	____
	________	____
	________	____
	________	____

List other goals and actions to be taken when the previous actions are successfully under way. Give approximate starting dates.

Goal	***Action***	***Starting Date***

ADDITIONAL READINGS

THIS SECTION CONTAINS suggested readings for topics covered in Chapters 1–10. Most of the books listed can be found in your public library or ordered from a nearby book store. Addresses are given for brochures and those books that need to be ordered directly from the organizations that produced them.

The National PTA has a number of publications on topics related to children's education, health and welfare, including *PTA Today,* a magazine for parents and PTA leaders. Brochures that were available when this book was written are listed under the appropriate chapter. Many of these brochures are also available in Spanish. For a copy of the current National PTA publications list, which includes information about how to order brochures or subscribe to *PTA Today,* send a self-addressed, stamped business-size envelope to Publications List, National PTA, Department D, 700 North Rush Street, Chicago, IL 60611–2571.

Two of the best books on education today are John Goodlad's *A Place Called School: Prospects for the Future*

(McGraw-Hill Book Company, 1984) and Ernest Boyer's *High School: A Report on Secondary Education in America* (Harper Colophon Books, 1983). Written by experts in the field, both books provide information about the state of education in America and what can be done to improve it.

Chapter 1: You Can Make a Difference

Anne Henderson's *The Evidence Continues to Grow: Parent Involvement Improves Student Achievement* (National Committee for Citizens in Education, 1987) surveys studies on the importance of parents being involved in their children's education. You can obtain information about books and brochures from the National Committee for Citizens in Education by writing to NCCE, Wilde Lake Village Green, Columbia, MD 21044.

What Works: Research About Teaching and Learning (Department of Education, 1986) provides practical information about how children learn. This booklet can be ordered from the Consumer Information Center, Pueblo, CO 81009.

Chapter 2: Getting Ready for School

David Elkind's *Miseducation: Preschoolers at Risk* (Alfred A. Knopf, 1987) is a provocative work by one of the best-known early childhood educators in America.

Getting Ready for School: What Kindergarten Teachers Would Like Your Child to Know (World Book, Inc., 1987) is a brochure that resulted from a survey of three thousand kindergarten teachers. For ordering information, write to World Book, P.O. Box 4140, Chicago, IL 60654.

National PTA brochures for parents of young children include *Children and TV: What Parents Can Do, Discipline: A*

Parent's Guide, Help Your Young Child Become a Good Reader and *Help Your Young Child Learn at Home.*

Chapter 3: Understanding Your Child's School

Tom and Harriet Sobel's series on *Your Child in School* presents a good overview of the curriculum in elementary schools as well as other useful information. Of the several books planned for this series, two have been published: *Kindergarten Through Second Grade* (Arbor House, 1987) and *The Intermediate Years: Grades Three Through Five* (Arbor House, 1987).

Rhoda Dersh's *School Budget: It's Your Money; It's Your Business* (National Committee for Citizens in Education, 1979) will help you get a general understanding of school budgets and the budget-making process.

David Schimmel and Louis Fischer's *Parents, Schools and the Law* (National Committee for Citizens in Education, 1987) answers many questions that parents have about their children's school records, and explains the legal rights of parents and their children in relation to the schools.

Chapter 4: How Is My Child Doing?

Ann Boehm and Mary Alice White's *The Parents' Handbook on School Testing* (Columbia Teachers College Press, 1982) and *Parents Can Understand Testing* (National Committee for Citizens in Education, 1980) will provide additional information about testing.

National PTA brochures include *Plain Talk About Tests*, prepared in conjunction with the Educational Testing Service (ETS), and *Making Parent-Teacher Conferences Work for Your Child,* prepared in conjunction with the National Education Association (NEA).

Chapter 5: Helping Your Child Learn

The RIF (Reading Is Fundamental) Guide to Encouraging Young Readers (Doubleday, 1987) provides two hundred reading activities and suggested books for children and parents.

The International Reading Association, 800 Barksdale Road, Newark, DE 19714; the American Library Association, 50 East Huron, Chicago, IL 60611; and RIF, Box 23444, Washington, DC 20026 have pamphlets with ideas for encouraging your child to read. Also see the National PTA brochures *Help Your Child Get the Most Out of Homework,* prepared in conjunction with NEA; *Help Your Young Child Become a Good Reader;* and *Children and TV: What Parents Can Do.*

Chapter 6: The Out-of-School Hours

Joan Bergstrom's *School's Out—Now What? Creative Choices for Your Child* (Ten Speed Press, 1984) will help you work with your child to find fun and productive activities.

David Elkind's *The Hurried Child: Growing Up Too Fast Too Soon* (Addison-Wesley, 1981) will remind you not to push your child into too many activities.

Lynette and Thomas Long's *The Handbook for Latchkey Children and Their Parents* (Arbor House, 1983) provides information about latchkey children, as does the National PTA brochure *Kids with Keys, Parents with Jobs.*

Chapter 7: The Needs of the Special Child

Kenneth Shore's *The Special Education Handbook: A Comprehensive Guide for Parents and Educators* (Columbia Teachers College Press, 1986) and Winifred Anderson, Stephen Chitwood and Deidre Hayden's *Negotiating the Special Education Maze* (Prentice-Hall Inc., 1982) are two of the many books that will help you understand special education.

Parents of gifted children will find these books of considerable interest: James Alvino and the editors of *Gifted Children Monthly*, *Parents' Guide to Raising a Gifted Child: Recognizing and Developing Your Child's Potential* (Little, Brown and Company, 1985) and Virginia Ehrlich, *Gifted Children: A Guide for Parents and Teachers* (Prentice-Hall, Inc., 1982).

Chapter 8: Keeping Kids Healthy

For further information about how to provide your child with a good sex education at home, see Sol Gordon's *Raising a Child Conservatively in a Sexually Permissive World* (Simon and Schuster, 1983) and Planned Parenthood's *How to Talk with Your Child About Sexuality: A Parent's Guide* (Doubleday, 1986).

There are also a number of useful books or pamphlets to read with your child or for her to read alone. Ask your local librarian or health teacher to help you find some appropriate ones. Recommended are Lynda Madaras's *What's Happening to My Body? Book for Boys: A Growing Up Guide for Parents and Sons* (Newmarket Press, 1987) and *What's Happening to My Body? A Growing Up Guide for Mothers and Daughters* (Newmarket Press, 1983).

National PTA brochures include *How to Talk to Your Child About Sex; How to Talk to Your Preteen and Teen About Sex; How to Talk to Your Teens and Children About AIDS; Alcohol, Drugs and Teens: What Parents Can Do; and Young Children and Drugs: What Parents Can Do.*

Chapter 9: Making Your Voice Heard

National PTA publications include *A Voice for Children and Youth: The National PTA Guide to Legislative Activity* and *Looking in on Your School: A Workbook for Improving Public Education.*

Chapter 10: Why Care About Other People's Children?

Harold Hodgkinson's *All One System: Demographics of Education, Kindergarten Through Graduate School* (Institute for Educational Leadership, 1985) is a brief, extremely valuable brochure that paints a graphic picture of the changing makeup of our schools and our nation. For information about how to obtain this brochure, write to: IEL, 1001 Connecticut Avenue NW, Washington, DC 20036.

INDEX

About the Author

Melitta J. Cutright is director of communications and programs for the National PTA in Chicago. She is the author of numerous articles, one of which won an EDPRESS award for outstanding feature story on education. Ms. Cutright holds a Ph.D. in history and is a former college professor. Her daughter, Elisabeth, entered kindergarten at her local public school in 1988.